Rebuilding community connections – mediation and restorative justice in Europe

by Ivo Aertsen, Robert Mackay, Christa Pelikan
Jolien Willemsens, Martin Wright

European Forum for Victim-Offender
Mediation and Restorative Justice
Leuven (Belgium)

Integrated project "Responses to violence in everyday life in a democratic society"

Council of Europe Publishing

French edition:

Renouer les liens sociaux – médiation et justice réparatrice en Europe

ISBN 92-871-5450-3

The views expressed in this publication are the authors' and do not necessarily reflect those of the Council of Europe.

All rights reserved. No part of this publication may be reproduced, stored in a retrieval system or transmitted, in any form or by any means – whether electronic (CD-Rom, Internet, etc.), mechanical, photocopying, recording or otherwise – without the prior permission of the Publishing Division, Directorate of Communication and Research.

Cover: *Elseneur* (1944), oil on canvas painting (73 cm by 60 cm)
René Magritte, private collection
@ Photothèque R. Magritte – ADAGP, Paris 2004

Design: Council of Europe Graphic Design Workshop

Council of Europe Publishing
F-67075 Strasbourg Cedex

ISBN 92-871-5451-1
© Council of Europe, July 2004
Printed in Germany

INTEGRATED PROJECT "RESPONSES TO VIOLENCE IN EVERYDAY LIFE IN A DEMOCRATIC SOCIETY"

All Europeans feel affected by violence and its repercussions. Personal security is threatened every day in a whole range of places and circumstances: at home, at school, at work, at sports events and on the streets. While violence and the fear of violence affect everyone's quality of life, certain groups – such as women, children and the elderly as well as migrants, refugees and particular ethnic groups – may be seen as specific targets.

The integrated project on "Responses to violence in everyday life in a democratic society" was launched by the Secretary General of the Council of Europe as a means of mobilising the Council's resources over a period of three years (2002-04) to address the widely shared concerns that violence engenders. Its main aim is to help decision makers and others to implement consistent policies of awareness-raising, prevention and law enforcement to combat violence in everyday life. Significantly, these policies have to be formulated and applied in ways that respect human rights and the rule of law. That is an absolute prerequisite for achieving lasting improvement in the actual situation and in people's feelings about security in Europe.

Rebuilding community connections – mediation and restorative justice in Europe is the ninth of a series of publications for a general and specialised readership containing recommendations or instruments used to launch Council of Europe activities and projects on violence prevention. The series also includes discussion and summary documents on the different topics covered by the integrated project.

Contents

Page

Foreword
Walter Schwimmer
Secretary General of the Council of Europe 7

Introduction 9

Chapter 1 – The background of mediation and restorative justice 11
- a. What is restorative justice? 11
- b. Development in Europe and beyond 16
- c. Mediation, conferencing and sentencing circles 18
- d. Types of crime and stages of the criminal justice process 21
- e. The restorative justice process and its working principles 26
- f. The need for an ethical framework 31
- g. What can we learn from empirical research? 34

Chapter 2 – Promoting and implementing mediation and restorative justice 41
- a. Committee of Ministers Recommendation No. R (99) 19 41
- b. The necessity of a legal framework and safeguards 46
- c. Organisational models 50
- d. Mediation and the community 53
- e. Training and education 54

Chapter 3 – How to set up mediation and restorative justice programmes 59
- a. Initiating a programme 59
- b. Acquiring funding 63
- c. Establishing co-operation 68

Chapter 4 – Restorative justice and its participants 71
- a. Volunteers and professionals 71
- b. Victim concerns 72
- c. Offender concerns 74
- d. Public opinion and the role of the media 76

Chapter 5 – Evaluation and further development 79
    a. Issues in programme evaluation and research 79
    b. Working toward comparability 85
    c. International co-operation 86

Appendix 91
    Committee of Ministers Recommendation No. R (99) 19 concerning mediation in penal matters 93
    Explanatory memorandum 97

References 115

Further reading 121

FOREWORD

Democratic society must respond to widespread concern about everyday violence and insecurity. In order to meet this difficult challenge effectively within the context of the rule of law and respect for individual human rights, appropriate instruments have to be developed. During the last few years, mediation has emerged as an instrument of choice for violence prevention and conflict management, and has thus become an important element in prevention programmes dealing with various forms of violence, such as in the family, in schools, in neighbourhoods and at sports events.

By giving a central place to the victim, restorative justice and mediation in penal matters can play an important role in managing the aftermath of violent acts.

Committee of Ministers Recommendation No. R (99) 19 concerning mediation in penal matters deals specifically with victim-offender mediation, and clearly sets out its definitions, procedures, conditions and limits. As this approach is relatively new and still little known to those likely to be involved in its implementation, I would strongly commend this handbook, which has been realised jointly by the Council of Europe's integrated project "Responses to violence in everyday life in a democratic society" and the European Forum for Victim-Offender Mediation and Restorative Justice. I am convinced it will contribute to the implementation of the recommendation.

Walter Schwimmer
Secretary General of the Council of Europe

INTRODUCTION

A growing number of European countries have introduced, in their criminal justice systems, new measures and approaches to crime, such as restorative justice (sometimes called victim-offender mediation or out-of-court offence resolution). In some, these new approaches are available throughout the whole country; in others they are only in their early stages. Countries in eastern Europe have expressed a particular interest in restorative justice.

Restorative justice is a new model of responding to criminal behaviour, balancing the needs of the victim, the offender and the community. The first of its three basic principles is that a society's response to crime should begin with repairing as much as possible the harm suffered by the victim. The second is that offenders should understand the effects of their act on their victim, and be encouraged to accept responsibility for it. The third is that the victim should have the opportunity to tell the offender directly about the effects of the offence, ask him or her questions, and then work out with the offender the best way to make reparation. There is scope for this process to be assisted by the participation of members of the community.

Restorative justice can avoid complicated, long-lasting formal criminal procedures, but it also raises new issues which need to be taken into account, some of which are considered in this book. It is only normal that this fairly new concept has given rise to different interpretations in different countries, but practical experience and research evidence have shown that it is most successful when the above-mentioned basic principles are adhered to.

To avoid the danger of restorative justice becoming a general term applied to various projects that lack some of its essential elements, the Committee of Ministers, the decision-making body of the Council of Europe, adopted in 1999 Recommendation No. R (99) 19 concerning mediation in penal matters (see appendix). This sets out the principles of victim-offender mediation and recommends that governments of the member states use them as guidelines. This initiative also formed the basis of a draft resolution of the United Nations Economic and Social Council in the following year. More recently, in 2001, the European Union issued a framework decision stating that member states should promote mediation in criminal cases and bring into force their legal instruments by 2006. Meanwhile the Council of Europe has promoted community-based sanctions and victim-offender mediation, followed up on the recommendation, and assisted with the training of mediators in eastern Europe.

In 2004, the Council, as part of its integrated project "Responses to violence in everyday life in a democratic society", decided to commission this guide to further support policy development and its implementation for restorative justice. It is intended to serve policy makers at all levels of government, judicial authorities and mediation services, together with their umbrella organisations. The European Forum for Victim-Offender Mediation and Restorative Justice was entrusted with this task.

The arrangement of the guide is as follows.

Chapter 1 gives the background of mediation and restorative justice. After explaining the concept, it outlines development in Europe and beyond. Some of the main types of restorative justice are described: victim-offender mediation, conferencing, and sentencing circles. There is a summary of restorative justice approaches for different types of crime and at different stages of the criminal justice process, followed by a brief account of how they function. The case is made for an ethical framework, and some of the main empirical research findings are summarised.

Chapter 2 is concerned with promoting and implementing mediation and restorative justice. The Council of Europe's Committee of Ministers Recommendation No. R (99) 19 is outlined, and some key issues are discussed. Other aspects include the necessity of a legal framework and safeguards, different organisational models for mediation, the relation of mediation to the community, and training and education.

Chapter 3 sets out ways of establishing mediation and restorative justice programmes, including motivating and mobilising the potential co-operating agencies and actors, acquiring funding, and establishing modes of co-operation.

In Chapter 4 some special issues are examined: the relative merits of using volunteers and professionals; victim concerns; offender concerns; and public opinion and the role of the media.

Finally Chapter 5 discusses evaluation and further development: the place of research in the development of restorative justice; working toward comparability; and international co-operation.

This guide deals with a new approach to criminal offences and does not take into account models of mediation in civil cases, such as family mediation or mediation in commercial disputes.

Unless otherwise stated, "mediation" will be used as a generic term including other models such as "conferencing" and "sentencing circles", and "mediator" will include those described with terms such as "facilitator".

The guide was written by a working group of the European Forum for Victim-Offender Mediation and Restorative Justice. Its contents are based on the experience of many people working in the European restorative justice area, including practitioners, policy makers and researchers. We are grateful for the input by many of them. Special thanks go to Torunn Bolstad for her support in the initial stage of the project.

CHAPTER 1

THE BACKGROUND OF MEDIATION AND RESTORATIVE JUSTICE

a. What is restorative justice?

Many expectations have been placed upon the criminal justice system and in recent years a new one has been added: it should focus more on victims. At the very least victims want to be kept informed of the progress (or lack of progress) of their case. If an accused person has been charged, they wish to know when the trial will take place. Surveys have shown that many of them would like to ask questions about the crime which only the offender can answer, and to tell him or her the effect it has had on their lives. Ideally, they would like the offender to make an apology, and some would also like some form of reparation. There have been repeated complaints that the criminal justice system ignores victims' needs and wishes in these matters.

In other words, the position of the victim of crime is largely overlooked, although some countries have introduced the idea of requiring offenders to pay monetary compensation to their victims. In France and Belgium, for example, this can be done through the *partie civile* procedure in parallel with a criminal trial, and in Germany through the (seldom used) *Adhäsionsverfahren* (a civil process "attached" to the criminal one). In England and Wales a civil action can be brought by the injured party quite independently of the criminal proceedings; criminal courts can also order the offender to pay compensation, and are required by law to consider doing so. When the crime has arisen from a dispute, for example a conflict between neighbours, it may be more important to them to resolve the conflict than to bring criminal charges and thus make continued co-existence impossible. Often in such cases the victim has also been at fault.

These considerations have also drawn attention to deficiencies in the way offenders are dealt with. They are normally represented by a lawyer, so that the accused often take very little part in their own trial. Procedural safeguards have been introduced in order to protect them against the risk of unjust punishment, but these can be exploited through procedural manoeuvres to secure a wrongful acquittal. Lawyers often try to deny the offence, or minimise the victim's pain and suffering, which is the opposite of what victims want. In this context, if the offender tries to apologise, it sounds like an attempt to escape punishment. If the punishment takes the form of imprisonment, it usually makes the payment of compensation impossible, and gives the offender a stigma which makes it harder to be re-integrated into the community. All too often it results in hardship to the offender's family and even the loss of their home. This does not encourage the offender to accept responsibility for the harm he or she has caused. Sometimes defence lawyers even try to blame the victim. The victim, however, wants the full seriousness of the harm to be acknowledged.

To overcome these difficulties, restorative justice approaches the event from a different point of view. Instead of focusing on the breaking of a law, and assuming that the response should be to punish the offender, it pays attention firstly to the persons who have been harmed. The first response is to try to repair the harm, as far as possible. If the offender is known, he or she is given the opportunity to make reparation (and if necessary required to do so). The victim is given the opportunity to ask questions and express feelings. The offender, in turn, is encouraged to acknowledge the harm, and to agree to make reparation. This idea is at the heart of restorative justice; it has been developed further in several ways, as will be seen below.

Restorative justice gives as much importance to the process as to the outcome. In the last thirty years concern has grown not only about the substance of the response to wrongdoing by the criminal justice system, but also about the procedure, especially the way in which victims of crime were treated, or rather ignored. Reporting a crime can be a time-consuming process. Victims are often not kept informed about the way their case is being dealt with. If the offender is detected, they may not be informed of the date the case will be heard in court. During the judicial investigation (or the trial in countries with a common-law system), those victims who are also witnesses see their role reduced to bringing or supporting evidence against the alleged offender. At the trial, victims can experience the debate (or the cross-examination by the defence lawyer in a common-law system) as if it were intended to make them appear to be lying, or at least unreliable. They are asked to answer questions related to the narrow problem of whether the offender is guilty or innocent. The whole process is not designed to allow victims to describe the background and the consequences of the case, let alone to ask questions themselves.

Victims want a less formal process, in which their views count; more information about the processing and outcome of their cases; to participate in their cases; to be treated respectfully and fairly; and to receive emotional and/or material restoration (the latter is relatively low on the list of priorities) (Strang, 2002). Victims experience a wide range of reactions to crime. At first they often feel shock and anger, and these feelings sometimes persist. There is evidence however that they are not as punitive as is sometimes assumed. The British Crime Survey, for example, found that for some quite serious crimes, such as burglary and robbery, twice as many victims wanted community sanctions as compared with those who wanted prison for their offenders (Mattinson and Mirrlees-Black, 2000). But a common response to this, as to other bad experiences, some of which result in traumas, is to want some good to follow the harm they have suffered; many victims want the offenders to make better use of their lives, especially after having met them.

Origins and development of restorative justice

In conventional criminal justice the questions are asked: "Who committed the offence against the law and what sanction should be imposed?" The primary response is punishment, which is intended to be painful or at least unpleasant for the offender. Its aim is either symbolic, expressing the amount of retribution appropriate to the seriousness of the crime, or instrumental, to deter others and the offender him or herself. A second aim is rehabilitative: to recognise pressures towards crime in the offender's life, such as homelessness or lack of emotional support, and to try to meet those needs. These responses are generally regarded as a spectrum from "hard" to "soft". Thirdly, a sentence may aim to protect the public by restriction of liberty (for example disqualification from certain activities, curfew) or imprisonment. These aims often overlap, so that it is difficult to know which has priority.

Restorative justice does not use this spectrum. It asks a different set of questions: "Who has been harmed? What can be done to repair the harm? and Who should do it?" The focus is thus on the victim's needs, although those of the offender should not be forgotten. Meeting the victim and making reparation may be hard for the offender, but it is not done because it is hard – but rather because it is a step towards making the situation better.

The idea that wrongdoing should be put right through compensation can be traced back through history in many cultures (see, for example, Schafer, 1960; Wright, 1996; Weitekamp, 2000). In the last three decades there has been a renaissance of this both in Europe and in North America. In the 1950s the English penal reformer Margery Fry campaigned for compensation by the state for victims of crimes of violence; this was introduced in the United Kingdom in 1964 (a year after New Zealand) and some other countries have followed. Meanwhile in the United States (Columbus, Ohio) in 1971 a city attorney (prosecutor) saw that people were acquiring a criminal record for offences such as assaults, threats or theft, as a result of disputes within a family or neighbourhood. He had seen how dispute resolution could work in the Van Der Hoeven Kliniek in the Netherlands, among highly disturbed psychiatric patients, and saw no reason why people in the community should not use the same techniques. A separate initiative took place in 1974 in Kitchener, Ontario, Canada, where a probation officer proposed that it would be more constructive to require two young men to meet their victims and make reparation, rather than punish them (Wright, 1996). This gave rise to the Victim-Offender Reconciliation Programme, which spread in Canada and the United States, and received visitors from several European countries. Nearly thirty years later, one of the two men himself became a volunteer with the programme. In the late 1960s and early 1970s, a debate also started in Europe on how the consequences of an offence could be faced and resolved by those immediately involved. In that period, concrete proposals for innovative projects were formulated in various European countries. From the beginning of the 1980s, mediation practices started in countries such as Norway and Austria, in a rather independent way from North American developments.

At this stage the process was called "victim-offender mediation" (or "victim-offender reconciliation"), but already a third element had been introduced: the community. Firstly, mediators in early victim-offender mediation services were volunteers, members of the community who had undergone basic training (see sections 2.d, 4.a). Secondly, it was recognised that crimes often harm the community as well as the victim, and some victims do not require individual reparation but wish to see offenders make amends by some form of service to the community.

A further development of the concept of restorative justice is the recognition that the majority of offenders are not detected, so that victims are unable to seek the benefit of mediation even if they wanted to. For them, the only kind of restorative justice is to provide some form of victim assistance, although there have been experiments with victim-offender groups involving other offenders who had committed similar offences (see below, section 1.b). In some countries the state compensates victims of violence, either with money, or by paying for necessary medical treatment or psychotherapy, when this is not available through the welfare state. Compensation for stolen or damaged property, however, is left to private insurance, but in some countries, the "safety net" of the welfare state can help where the loss has caused severe hardship.

At this point some clarification is needed. Descriptions of restorative justice are commonly presented on the basis that an individual offender has harmed an individual victim. It should be remembered, however, that many crimes have no individual victim (for example criminal damage in a public place); also, some crimes are committed against organisations ("legal persons"), such as shops, clubs or schools, and others are committed by organisations, such as firms which falsify their accounts and factories which break laws on health and safety or pollute the environment. These can also be dealt with restoratively, as the Australian criminologist John Braithwaite (2002) has shown, by finding the right person in an organisation to represent it. For the sake of simplicity, only cases involving individual victims and offenders are dealt with here.

The defining features of restorative justice are that the starting point is repair of the harm associated with crime, and that victims and offenders have the opportunity to discuss the offence and appropriate reparation. They are the "owners" of the conflict, as Professor Nils Christie of Norway has suggested, and it should not be "stolen" from them by professionals such as lawyers and social workers (Christie, 1977). A further dimension is the involvement of members of the community in the process: it has been suggested that this can not only contribute to finding a good outcome for each individual case, but can help people to understand the pressures leading to crime, so that they can be addressed.

One definition of restorative justice has been proposed by the Restorative Justice Consortium (1998) in the United Kingdom:

> Restorative justice seeks to balance the concerns of the victim and the community with the need to re-integrate the offender into society. It seeks to assist the recovery of the victim and enable all parties with a stake in the justice process to participate fruitfully in it.

Emphasis is placed on the acceptance by the accused of responsibility for causing harm, even if acceptance does not mean full legal guilt. The process has been compared to the Truth and Reconciliation Commissions in South Africa and elsewhere: by removing the threat of punishment for those who accept responsibility for their actions, they make it easier for the accused to admit those actions and to understand the hurt caused to the victims. For many victims this acknowledgement is more important than retribution, and it enables their communities to accept the offender and make a new beginning. Of course this ideal process does not happen in every case, but it appears to be more successful than a confrontational process in promoting social integration.

The basic theory of restorative justice has been summarised by Howard Zehr (1995; 2002), one of the earliest practitioners and thinkers on the subject. The starting point is that crime causes harm to victims, and that the offender therefore has an obligation to try to make things right. Restorative justice promotes the engagement or participation of all parties – victims, offenders and community – in this process. Also important are the "how" – the process of dialogue by which the situation is resolved should itself be restorative; and the "who" – the involvement of the "stakeholders", the members of the community affected by crime, and the "communities of care" who can support the victim and the offender. Addressing the harm caused by the crime makes it necessary to provide the services which victims and offenders need; the victim-offender dialogue is not sufficient on its own. It is also necessary to address the pressures that lead to crime: most victims "want to know that steps are being taken to reduce such harms to themselves and others" (Zehr, 2002: 29). In some cases, however, the necessary steps may involve additional personal or financial commitment on the part of other members of society, in order to ensure that these steps are taken.

It can be seen from the above that restorative justice can be more readily described than defined. There are also difficulties in translating the term into some languages. In Latin languages, the words equivalent to "restorative" have the connotation of restoring property to its owner, but also restoring an injured person to health or a damaged article to its former condition. In German, *wiedergutmachend* (making good again) tends to be used for "restitution", financial reparation. *Wiederherstellend* is less often used, but may be closer to the meaning. There is a similar distinction between the Polish *zadośćuczynienie* (satisfaction) and *naprawczy* (reparative) which is now the preferred term. In Russian, there is a debate about whether to translate "justice" as *pravosudie* (the machinery of imposing judgements), or *spravedlivost'* (being just). It is suggested that *pravosudie* should be used for the judicial process, and *spravedlivost'* for the way of reaching a just outcome.

There is also the question of "criminal justice" and "criminal law". Some countries use the term "penal law", because the expectation is that those who break the law will be punished, although in the late 19th century the idea was introduced that, for many offenders, assistance and support were more likely than punishment to lead them to avoid re-offending. In French, for example, the term is *droit pénal*, in German *Strafrecht*, in Dutch *strafrecht* (penal law). Similarly, "victim-offender mediation" is commonly translated into French as *médiation pénale* (and corresponding words in other Latin languages). This is, however, incorrect, because mediation is not punitive. *Médiation en matière pénale* does not avoid the problem; we suggest that the term used by the United Nations, *médiation en matière criminelle*, would be more appropriate.

b. Development in Europe and beyond

Restorative justice is a worldwide movement. It was born, or re-born, in Europe and North America in the 1970s, as has been described above, but it has drawn on age-old traditions from Africa, Latin America and Asia, and First Nations in Canada and New Zealand (Christie, 1977; Stevens, 2000).

Conflict regulation of some kind has been an essential part of human societies from hunter-gatherers onwards. In Roman law only wrongs against the state or religion were generally prosecuted; others were mostly dealt with by the parties themselves under civil law (for a detailed overview see Hartmann, 1995). In medieval times too the idea of a wrong to a person or clan was primary, and that of an offence against the common good was secondary (Wright, 1996).

Major religions emphasise reparation to varying degrees, although some also give a place to retribution. In Buddhism "[f]ollowing the rules well is not in itself the goal; the reason for rules is that they promote personal and spiritual development". If the state uses violence, it reinforces the belief that violence works; wrongdoing is followed not by punishment imposed by others but by karma, its effect on ourselves. Islam makes many references to mercy and forgiveness, and includes provision for reconciliation and compensation.[1] The Judaeo-Christian Old Testament also gives a mixed picture, with some retributive rules, but others stressing the re-establishment of *shalom*, a state of material well-being, social relationships and ethical conduct; the Christian New Testament instructs: "Do not return evil for evil, but drive out evil with good" (Zehr, 1995).

Aspects of the restorative ideal are found in many cultures. In some cases the most distinguishing feature is the informal, deliberative process of justice. The outcome is often decided by arbitration, rather than mediation, by a group of elders, but usually after hearing from the parties and other members of the community. The example given by Nils Christie in his much-quoted article "Conflicts as property" (1977) comes from Arusha, Tanzania, where the community-based moot has aspects of arbitration by lay judges as well as the possibility of participation by the parties themselves. From South Africa comes the spirit of *ubuntu*, "the healing of breaches, the redressing of imbalances, the restoration of broken relationships" (Tutu, 1999). In Uganda, although the procedure is still informal and uses customary as well as statute law, the local council courts have been formalised by statute; the remedies granted by the courts include reconciliation, compensation, restitution[2] and apology, although more coercive measures are also available in some

---

1. For an outline of restorative aspects of major religions, see Hadley, 2001.
2. In this guide the terms "restitution" and "reparation" will be used interchangeably.

cases. Similarly in South Asia there are *panchayats* (councils of about five people) and more recent adaptations such as the *lok adalat* (people's court) in Rangpur, Gujarat, in which the complainant and respondent nominate representatives to negotiate a decision; failing that, the chairperson decides. Not all of these initiatives are restorative, however – they may include banishment or spearing, for example – and some have encountered problems associated with informal justice, such as lack of training of members of the *panchayat*, doubts about their appointment procedure, and delays and postponements which discourage participants from travelling from sometimes distant villages (Stevens, 2000).

Other examples, which have been influential in western countries, are the traditions of the Maori in New Zealand, which have been incorporated into family group conferences for juveniles, and those of First Nations in Canada and the United States which have inspired the idea of sentencing circles. These will be described below (see section 1.e).

In Europe, towards the end of the 20th century, the idea had developed in different ways in various countries.[1] Only a selection can be mentioned here. The first project in Norway, in 1981, inspired by Nils Christie, was originally seen as an alternative to imprisonment for juveniles, and then as a contribution to the care of youngsters with behavioural problems. Two years later the Ministry of Social Affairs began to encourage local governments to establish similar programmes, extended to adults in 1989. In 1991 the extension of the programme throughout the country for a broad range of offences was authorised under the civil division of the Ministry of Justice. Today, trained voluntary mediators are used, as in Finland and France, and this can have a social-educational effect.

Another European country to have victim-offender mediation established nationwide by law is Austria, where it is organised by full-time mediators in the semi-autonomous organisation Neustart, which runs a range of criminal-law related services. Mediation started as a pilot project for juveniles. It became part of the new Juvenile Justice Act of 1988 and was later extended to adults.

In France, after the introduction of Boîtes Postales 5000 (PO Boxes 5000) to resolve disputes between consumers and traders in 1976, the idea of mediation in criminal matters was taken up by the victim assistance movement and by some magistrates. In 1984 there were initiatives in Valence and Grenoble, which used existing law to employ mediation as one way of repairing the harm suffered by victims. Similarly the Institut national d'aide aux victimes et de médiation (Inavem) was established at a conference of victim assistance organisations in 1986. Eventually in 1993 the position was regularised by a law amending the Code of Criminal Procedure, and in 1998 the payment of legal aid fees facilitated access to victim-offender mediation. Much of the mediation is carried out by volunteers (Bonafé-Schmitt, 1992). In Germany it was the biennial congress of lawyers that

---

1. In this section, unless stated otherwise, descriptions of countries are taken from: European Forum for Victim-Offender Mediation and Restorative Justice (ed.) (2000) *Victim-offender mediation in Europe: making restorative justice work*, Leuven, Leuven University Press, and Lauwaert, K. and Aertsen, I. (2002) "Restorative justice: activities and expectations at European level", ERA Forum: scripta iuris europaei, (1), 27-32.

recommended the idea in 1984; pilot projects were initiated at first by the court assistance service, under existing law, and by independent associations such as Die Waage (The Scales) in Hannover and Handschlag (Handshake) in Reutlingen. The Criminal Code was amended to include victim-offender mediation in 1994. Belgium has, since the 1990s, developed several programmes, including some working with adults and some which deal with serious offences, and now has a restorative justice adviser in every prison.

In England and Wales the first projects for both juveniles and adults in the early 1980s were inspired by American models. The movement developed slowly until the 1990s, when a renaissance took place modelled on experiences in New Zealand and Australia. There have been other projects for categories of persons whose needs deserve greater attention, namely victims whose offenders are not known, and offenders whose victims do not wish to take part in mediation. One of these is based on "victim awareness", in which a probation officer or perhaps someone who has previously been a victim encourages offenders to think about the effects of their crime on the victims. In another experiment, groups of offenders met victims of similar offences; this can be enlightening for both, but requires careful facilitation (Launay and Murray, 1989). More recently there have been projects using "circles of support", groups of volunteers who support sexual offenders on their release from prison. In Poland, a visit to Germany by Patronat, a group concerned with prisoners' welfare, and the Senate Intervention Office, led to the formation of a committee to introduce victim-offender mediation, and eventually to the appointment of several hundred mediators by courts of appeal and by authorised institutions. A Polish Centre for Mediation has been established, which, with other organisations, organises training, and is working towards ensuring that all mediators, for adult cases as well as juveniles, are trained.

Other European countries have carried out experiments or initiated nationwide developments in victim-offender mediation as well. They include, amongst others, Denmark, Finland, Sweden, Ireland, the Netherlands, Luxembourg, Switzerland, Albania, Slovenia, Czech Republic, Bulgaria, Italy and Spain.

There are also wide variations in legislation, as will be seen in section 2.b, but the examples above show how the concept of mediation has taken root in different countries according to their laws, traditions, and the inspiration of individuals and organisations which have worked to preserve and extend the new philosophy. The European Forum for Victim-Offender Mediation and Restorative Justice has taken a lead in promoting exchanges of information and experience, with an emphasis on restorative justice as a practical method of responding to crime.

c. Mediation, conferencing and sentencing circles

There is a variety of methods for putting restorative justice into practice, including victim-offender mediation, conferencing, and sentencing circles. A fuller account of them is given in section 1.e.

Victim-offender mediation usually involves a one-to-one meeting between the victim and the offender, although someone may come with them to provide support, especially in the case of juveniles. It is facilitated by a mediator (or sometimes two). In some countries a face-to-face meeting is the norm; in others, victims who do not wish to meet "their" offender are offered indirect ("shuttle" or "pendulum") mediation, in which the mediators take messages between them. This can lead to an agreement, but is less likely to produce the feelings of empathy which can be a valuable feature of mediation.

Victim-offender conferencing (also known as "community conferencing"), often used with juvenile offenders, is similar, but more people are present: the young person's extended family are invited, and often another person who has a good rapport with the ofender, such as a sports teacher or club leader. The victim and a supporter, or others affected by the crime, are also invited to take part. Experience with adults is growing, and the supporters are more likely to include people from outside the family.

Family group conferencing, started in New Zealand, also includes the offender's family and the victim, but in addition professionals from agencies involved with the offender take part. It is a model used mainly for young people in trouble who are known to many agencies.

Sentencing circles are still more inclusive; they may include members of the community. The most significant difference from the other models, however, is that the judge and prosecutor are present. This method has been used in Canada, especially (but not only) by some judges working among First Nation peoples. It has not, to our knowledge, been applied in Europe, although demonstrations have taken place.[1]

In Europe, the most commonly used form is victim-offender mediation, which may be illustrated through two short case histories. The first example comes from Austria.

> In the Prater (an amusement park in Vienna), two young men on their way back from some well-lubricated merriment, "took" a motor vehicle to get home. The vehicle broke down and the police caught the youngsters while they were pushing it along. Its owner, a young Pakistani newspaper seller (a dangerous and low-paid job selling newspapers at the side of the road) was aggrieved by the loss of his vehicle, which was essential for his job. The mediator got in contact first with the two young men and afterwards with the victim, who in the beginning was reluctant, even defensive, to talk about ways of arranging compensation. The two boys said that the vehicle had been in poor condition anyway and that compensation payments ought to be reduced accordingly. When the mediation session, in which the mediator was also present, took place at last, the confrontation became very intense. The offenders appeared disconcerted and deeply impressed by the dreary picture which the newspaper seller drew of the circumstances of his life and work. An agreement about compensation payments was reached; it was a compromise between the victim's first demand and the offenders' first offer, to be paid in three instalments. The state prosecutor dropped the indictment.

---

1. A video recording of one of these is available from the Restorative Justice Consortium, London.

The following case comes from the Belgian Mediation for Redress Programme.

> At closing time, two shopkeepers (husband and wife) were threatened and robbed by two men using fake pistols and wearing balaclavas. Although the shopkeepers were beaten and knocked to the ground, the robbers were not able to get away with the days' takings. The day after, they were arrested by the police and one of them, who had reached the age of majority, was remanded in custody for one month. The case was referred to the local mediation service by the public prosecutor. The mediation services contacted the victims and the offenders, including their parents. For several weeks there was intensive communication between the mediator and all the parties. The offenders' lawyers were contacted as well, mainly concerning financial compensation for the material and psychological damages. Because the victims felt too much anxiety and agitation, a direct, face-to-face meeting between victims and offenders could not take place. However, both victims and offenders wanted to know about the other side. Therefore, the mediation continued on an indirect basis with the mediator acting as a go-between. He communicated questions and answers, feelings and concerns. The way the offence occurred and the use of violence were discussed in the light of the experience of both parties. The shopkeepers did not understand the motives of the young men, who apparently – because of their social background and studies – had no reason to commit the crime at all. Both men explained how they had prepared the hold-up, and that they had done it mainly for the kick. They also had the chance to explain to the victims the consequences of their enterprise for themselves, amongst other things in relation to their studies and prospects, the effects on their families and the reactions from their friends, who were now avoiding them. The victims could make clear how they felt and how the offence had changed their daily life, for example how they experienced a tendency to distrust customers and how they felt anxious each night when they left the store. They also communicated to the offenders their expectations and feelings about the judicial process, and a discussion with the offenders emerged on what a reasonable reaction by the court could be in this case. Finally, a written agreement was signed by all parties, which dealt not only with the financial compensation, but also included some of the other information that was exchanged during the mediation, for example on feelings, needs and expectations.

These cases show several things about the restorative process. Mediation implies the accused's admission of involvement in the alleged offence, although in most jurisdictions an admission of legal *guilt* is not required. The process should be voluntary on both sides. Although the offender's choice is limited, often between mediation and prosecution, for example, it is a choice, and this is necessary if the victim is to feel that any apology is sincere. If the accused denies causing any harm, the charge has to be tested in court – although that does not rule out a restorative intervention at a later stage, as will be seen below (section 1.d). As is shown by the second example, indirect mediation is a good alternative in case a direct encounter between the parties is not feasible. In both direct and indirect mediation a process based on problem-solving and understanding rather than punishment can encourage open discussion. Among other points, not shown by these particular cases, mediation can be used with a corporate "victim" (a "legal person") if the firm has an imaginative representative. Reparation can be effective without being punitive. The community can be involved in the process, and may share some responsibility for allowing the offence to happen.

Methods and principles applied in the mediation process will be given in section 1.e.

d. Types of crime and stages of the criminal justice process

Types of crimes

Restorative methods can be used at any stage of the criminal justice process, and at least to some extent, for crimes of any degree of seriousness, as stated in the Council of Europe recommendation. There is some evidence that mediation and conferencing work better with relatively serious crimes, where the victim has strong feelings that need to be resolved. Furthermore, mediations and especially conferences are time-consuming to arrange, which is another reason for investing resources primarily in the more serious cases. The seriousness, however, should be assessed not only on the basis of legal categories but also according to the effect on the victim and other people involved and their needs. If an apparently minor crime, such as burglary in which little was stolen, has a serious effect on the victim, then mediation should be considered. The earlier in the criminal justice process the case is referred to mediation, the more speedily it will be dealt with. This is normally an advantage (provided that the victim is not asked to make a decision before he or she is ready) and saves time in the criminal justice process. However, the more serious the offence, the more persuasion is needed on the part of lawyers, victim advocates or the mediation service to persuade the prosecutor or judge to refer the case to mediation. Lastly, it has been found in many countries that it is easier to obtain acceptance of restorative methods for juvenile offenders; this is understandable, but a fully restorative system must include adults as well, because a victim should not be excluded from it merely because the offender has passed his or her 18th birthday.

Crimes of violence are not necessarily excluded; the criterion is rather whether an individual victim or offender appears likely to be physically or verbally violent, or overbearing, so that a meeting could be damaging. There is debate as to whether offences where the victim is vulnerable are suitable for mediation. Many practitioners consider that they are, provided that the mediators conduct the proceedings in such a way as to protect them from possible physical or psychological damage, and from accepting unsatisfactory agreements. In Austria, for example, cases of domestic violence are referred to mediation, but this is always conducted by a male/female pair of mediators who have received special training.

Stages

Mediation can occur:

1. independently from the criminal justice system;
2. when referred by the police or prosecutors at pre-court stage, or by the judge before the main hearing (diversionary models);
3. parallel to prosecution;
4. after conviction and before sentencing;
5. as part of and/or in addition to a non-custodial sentence;
6. in prison: post-sentence or pre-release.

Independently from the criminal justice system. Two categories of cases deserve special mention. The first is where the victim and the offender know each other. Many crimes, including the most serious, are the outcome of a dispute between neighbours, colleagues at work, or people who knew each other in some other context. This can lead to violence against property, or an attack on the other person. Often it is impossible to say who was the offender and who the victim: one person may behave in a way that is annoying or provocative, but not criminal, and refuse to stop, driving the other to retaliate in a way that is criminal. Here it can make more sense to enable them to resolve the underlying dispute, rather than to classify the act as a crime. Better still is to provide a neighbourhood mediation service which offers the possibility of resolving such cases before feelings run too high.

The second concerns incidents in schools. Many of these could be classified as crimes: fights, extortion of pocket money, violent bullying, and so on, but can be dealt with by mediation. Schools generally do not report such incidents to the police, but they often attempt to deal with them by methods which mimic the criminal justice system: the victim is expected to report the offence to the school authorities, who deal with it by punishment. However, the same problems are encountered as on the outside, perhaps more intensely in the enclosed community of the school. Victims do not dare to report the incident for fear of retaliation by the offender, or if they do, the offender may be stigmatised and even excluded from school. Schools in some countries, such as Germany, French-speaking parts of Belgium, England and Northern Ireland, have begun to introduce peer mediation, for which the term "restorative justice" is sometimes used. School students (including primary level) are selected for training as mediators (and these are not necessarily the best-behaved students); after training and assessment, they are designated as mediators, and other school students with conflicts are encouraged to go to them, rather than to teachers. The school makes available a room where training and mediation can take place, and a member of staff who will support the mediators by discussing any difficulties they experience.

Both of these are methods that not only enable cases to be kept out of the criminal justice system, but have the potential to leave both parties on speaking terms, or at least not in fear of each other.

Referral by police or by prosecutors at the pre-court stage, or by the judge before the main hearing (diversionary models). Probably the system which has embraced restorative justice most comprehensively is the juvenile justice system in New Zealand, where it is used for all types of cases except homicide. The law is clear: "unless the public interest requires otherwise, criminal proceedings should not be instituted against a child or young person if there is an alternative means of dealing with the matter" (Children, Young Persons and their Families Act 1989, section 308(a)). An estimated 80%-85% of cases are dealt with by a formal police warning, or an informal police caution with tasks (with the agreement of the young person, his or her parents and the victim) such as community work and payment of restitution. Most of the rest are dealt with by a family group conference; they go to court only if no agreement is reached or if the offence is arrestable (see "after conviction before the sentence" below) (McElrea, 1998).

In England and Wales, where the discretionary principle also applies, police have the option in certain cases of administering a reprimand or a final warning. The final warning may be accompanied by rehabilitative measures or mediation. Thames Valley Police have changed the earlier idea, in which a warning consisted of a threat of serious consequences if bad behaviour was repeated; instead they now emphasis the harmful effects on the victim. This is known as a "restorative caution"; or if the victim is present, a "restorative conference". The process has been evaluated (see section 1.g). The police can issue a "caution" to adults, and the government's Criminal Justice Act 2003 provides a statutory basis for "conditional cautions" accompanied by rehabilitative or reparative measures. This is due to begin in 2004 (Home Office, 2003). Police referrals to an (external) mediation service frequently take place in Finland and Norway as well. In Belgium, projects in close co-operation with police services have been set up in several localities; the mediator mostly functions as a municipal civil servant, and he or she is sometimes part of the police service. The Netherlands also has a few experimental restorative justice projects with some local police services. In Scotland, the public prosecutor can refer a case to a mediation service using the power of discretion inherent in the Crown Prerogative. The Children's Reporter can refer a child or young person to a mediation service using statutory powers of discretion.

Prosecutors are the main source of referrals to mediation in most European countries in which the principle of opportuneness[1] (appropriateness) is followed. Even some of those which use the mandatory prosecution (legality) principle have modified their practice to allow this: in Germany, for example, the "requirement to prosecute" *(Anklagezwang)* was modified in 1975 by the principle of opportuneness *(Opportunitätsprinzip)* which allows the prosecutor discretion to discontinue prosecution of minor offences and impose certain measures, including compensation or work for the community (Code of Criminal Procedure, section 153a). This has the additional advantage of saving the court's time by avoiding trial. In 1994, the Criminal Code (section 46a) was also amended to allow the court to mitigate or omit punishment if the offender has made good his or her action completely or very substantially through efforts to reach agreement with the injured party.

When the prosecution is initially only deferred, not halted, this provides a spur to the offender to complete reparation as agreed. In Italy, the trial of a juvenile can be suspended, with probation, to allow the young person to do voluntary work or other activities of social utility, or mediation.[2] The legality principle (mandatory prosecution) may make it difficult for the case to be diverted out of the system in this way before it has reached the court. Prosecutors, however, can make enquiries about a young offender during investigation, and in several countries there are

---

1. The term "opportuness", also reffered to as opportunity, is used in the sense of "the quality of being opportune or appropriate", in other words allowing for the exercise of discretion.
2. Article 28, Decree of the President of the Republic 448/89, cited by Baldry et al., 1998, 377-378.

mediation services to which they can send the case for evaluation. If the outcome is positive, the judge dismisses the case, with the advantage that the offender has had to face the consequences of his or her act, and the victim has had the opportunity to express feelings and obtain answers to questions. Even with the legality principle still in place, courts can refer certain types of (less serious) cases to mediation, and for complainant offences such as insults, an attempt at conciliation is mandatory (Trujillo, 2000).

In England and Wales, courts must refer juvenile first offenders (with certain exceptions) to a youth offending panel, composed of one staff member and two trained volunteers. They hold a hearing at which the victim may be present, as well as supporters for both victim and offender; the aim is to require the offender to undertake various constructive activities, including reparation if required. So far, however, few victims have taken part.

Parallel to prosecution. In some countries, restorative justice projects have been developed parallel to prosecution. This means that mediation is offered when the public prosecutor has already decided to prosecute the suspect. The Belgian Mediation for Redress Programme is an example of this approach. This programme focuses in particular on more serious crimes. The mediation is done by an independent mediation service, normally in close co-operation with other victim-offender mediation services of the judicial district. When a written agreement in mediation is reached, this is added to the judicial file, and can thereby influence the further sentencing process carried out by the public prosecutor and the judge.

After conviction and before the sentence. In common-law countries, conviction (finding of guilt) and sentence (imposition of sanction) are two separate stages in the criminal justice process. After conviction the case is often adjourned for about three weeks, so that the probation service can prepare a pre-sentence report. The possibility of mediation can be explored during this time, and may be included in the report to the court. In England and Wales, the court can postpone the sentence for a maximum of six months to see whether the offender makes, or at least begins to make, reparation. The sentence is not decided until the end of the period of deferment, and the expectation is that it will be non-custodial.

As part of and/or in addition to a non-custodial sentence. In the New Zealand juvenile justice system, arrestable offences (those in which an arrest is necessary to prevent absconding, further offending or interference with evidence) are sent to court; then, at the stage where before the 1989 Act a pre-sentence report would have been provided, the case is referred to a conference. It then returns to the court, where the judge in most cases endorses the agreement reached. This is usually a plan of action including, for example, reparation, community work, curfew and/or attending school or not associating with co-offenders. Sometimes it includes a sanction, if the offender and his or her family feel that this is unavoidable. Recommendations of family group conferences are accepted by the judge in 80% of cases, but sometimes the youth court can impose up to three months in a social welfare institution followed by six months' supervision, or the court can convict and refer the young person to the district court for sentence, which can include imprisonment for up to five years. When the act came into force in 1989, there was a sharp drop in the number of young people sent to prison (McElrea, 1998). European countries are only beginning to experiment with family group conferences, but research findings from New Zealand and Australia are very encouraging (see Morris and Maxwell, 2003; Strang, 2002).

In England and Wales, probation officers should include, as part of a probation order (now known as a community rehabilitation order) a short programme to make offenders aware of the victim's point of view. In some cases, after an offender has completed this module, mediation may be suggested by the probation officer or by the offender. In some areas victims are being made aware of this and can also request mediation.

In some countries courts have issued orders which require the offender to take part in mediation. It is better to refer the case to the mediation service first, so that they can assess the suitability of the case. They should make sure that the victim is taking part voluntarily, and that the offender can make an informed choice (see also section 2.a below).

In prison: post-sentence or pre-release. Some countries, such as Belgium, England and Wales, and the Netherlands, are beginning to introduce restorative processes in prison. The pilot project "Mediation for Redress" *(herstelbemiddeling)* in the Netherlands is dealing with the most serious crimes, including homicide and armed robbery by professional offenders. This type of mediation is usually focused on the psychological needs of both parties. It may happen at any stage of the prison sentence. In some ways it is beneficial to arrange it relatively soon. In other cases mediation can be offered before the offender's release. The victim, the offender, or both may be afraid of being attacked by the other (or friends or relatives) if the prisoner returns to the same community, and if they can reach an understanding to avoid that, the offender's re-integration will be helped. Mediation should, however, only be introduced in prisons when there is already adequate provision for it in the community. It would be unfortunate if the availability of different kinds of services within the prison were used to legitimate the judge's decision to impose a prison sentence. The same applies to community service undertaken by prisoners (such as repairing wheelchairs or transcribing Braille). If it is unavoidable that an offender be sent to prison, it is of course highly desirable that he or she should be able to undertake constructive work of this kind. But courts should be aware that it is only available to a minority of prisoners, and the question should always be asked: "Could they not undertake it in the community, avoiding all the well-known harmful side-effects of imprisonment (not to mention the cost)?"

The prison itself may be the locus for conflict resolution activities and mediation. These interventions may be used to deal with problems and conflicts arising within the prison community: between prisoners, between prisoners and staff, and between staff.

e. The restorative justice process and its working principles

This section gives a brief account of the three main restorative justice processes, and then summarises some of their common features, elements of the process and the working principles of empowerment and recognition.

Below are examples of the basic principles summarised by the United Nations, which uses a restorative process or aim to achieve a restorative outcome. According to the United Nations (2002):

> A "restorative process" means any process in which the victim, the offender and/or any other individuals or community members affected by a crime actively participate together in the resolution of matters arising from the crime, often with the help of a fair and impartial third party. Examples of restorative processes include mediation, conferencing and sentencing circles.
>
> "Restorative outcome" means an agreement reached as a result of a restorative process. Examples of restorative outcomes include restitution, community service and any other programme or response designed to accomplish reparation of the victim and the community, and reintegration of the victim and/or the offender.

Victim-offender mediation

To start with, both the offender and the victim should be interviewed separately, to establish whether there is any reason why mediation should not proceed, such as a risk of physical or verbal violence on either side. The offender is in many cases interviewed first, so as not to raise the victim's expectations where mediation is not considered appropriate.

The visits/interviews may lead to a mediation session, which should be in a neutral place such as a community centre, not the victim's or offender's home, and preferably not a place associated with authority such as a court building. Both victim and offender attend, sometimes each with a supporter who does not take part in the proceedings (or does so only partly, mainly for the settlement of specific questions of financial compensation).

There exist different methodological approaches depending on the type of offence at stake and on the specific victim-offender relationship. In Austria, for example, several methods or settings have been developed to deal with different constellations:

- standard method: before direct mediation takes place, the mediator invites the offender and the victim to separate interviews. If both agree to search for a common out-of-court solution, the mediation session proper takes place. This is the approach used most frequently;
- a special type of mediation is used in cases where no individual victim is available, for example in cases of racist incidents. There a substitute (surrogate) is used to take over the victim's role. This representative might be a person from the victim's (ethnic) community or a social worker who takes over the role of the "other";
- mixed double, two co-mediators (one male and one female): this setting, initially designed for conflicts between partners, is now also used for other forms

of conflicts in close relationships, for example in the (extended) family. It also starts with a separate interview. The mediators then retell the stories they have heard in a session of four (the two mediators and the two parties). At first the conflict partners just listen, then they begin discussing their problem. A special technique used in the course of the mixed double is the "reflecting team". The mediators exchange their impressions and thoughts with regard to the process to each other, in the presence of the concerned couple, who just listen. In England and Wales, where parties come from different ethnic backgrounds, mediators from similar backgrounds may be chosen if available;

– tandem: no separate interview takes place but the session starts with victim (or offender) telling their story to the mediator while the offender (or victim) is sitting behind him or her so that they cannot see each other. If an agreement to continue victim-offender mediation is reached, a triangular dialogue *(Dialog im Dreieck)* is arranged. The conversation is still limited to one of the conflict partners and the mediator; the other partner is just listening. A direct mediation session will be held only if a basis for constructive conflict resolution can be established.

– *staffelrad* (relay cycle): this method is used when working with groups of offenders. Again, separate interviews take place, first with the victim, then with the group. If the group is willing to take responsibility, a mediation session is held. One offender after the other meets the victim and apologises. In the end, all the involved persons gather to talk about reparation (Altweger and Hitzl, 2001, 51-60).

Although details vary, victim-offender mediation has the following aims and takes the following course.

The process aims to empower (see below) two people – one who has suffered the harm and one who has caused it – by providing an opportunity to talk about it in a non-threatening atmosphere, so that each can express their own feelings and listen to the other's. The offender is asked to confirm that he or she took part in the action which caused the harm (see also 2.b). The victim, and then the offender, are each asked to make a short statement describing what happened, without interruption from the other. The victim's needs for reparation, both financially and emotionally, ought to be addressed and the offender is asked to propose and offer adequate ways of compensating the victim and of offering an authentic and acceptable apology. It is left to them to decide the outcome: whether the victim wants reparation, or is content with an apology, and in which way the offender is willing and able to make amends.

Very often a written agreement is reached that is laid before the agencies of the criminal justice system and whose fulfilment is monitored by either the victim-offender mediation services or the criminal-justice system agencies.

Conferencing

A type of conference which can be used for welfare issues as well as offending is the family group conference (FGC) developed in New Zealand. The method was originally introduced in 1989 for juveniles who have welfare needs to discuss these with their families; when they have committed an offence, the victim (also with supporters) can take part as well. A specific procedure, designed to be sensitive to traditions of the indigenous Maori people, was laid down in the Children, Young Persons and their Families Act 1989. A similar model is followed in some places in England and Wales, sometimes organised by the local youth offending team (YOT), a multi-disciplinary team of representatives of the main criminal justice agencies and the social services, health and education authorities. Members of the young person's extended family are invited to attend the family group conference.

The procedure may be described by means of the following case history (all names and some details have been changed).

> Robert, aged 14, had indecently assaulted Laura, his sister's best friend. He stopped as soon as she became upset. Laura told Robert's mother, who calmed her and told Robert off. At that time Laura wanted to forget it, but later she told her father (the parents of both children were separated). Robert and his parents were visited several times, and he was considered suitable to take part in a family group conference. Laura and her mother were also visited; at first they refused, but after a fortnight they decided to attend the FGC. Present were: Laura and her mother, Robert and his father, Robert's mentor, an education worker from the YOT, and two facilitators. The ground rules and the four-part structure of the session were explained and agreed: (1) First, was the victim/offender dialogue. After Robert had confirmed that he did not deny the offence, the effects on all concerned were discussed. Laura and her mother made powerful statements about the impact of the offence at that time, since then, at present, and what they wanted in the future. (2) Then a representative of youth offending team explained the official requirements, and relevant support agencies. (3) After this, everyone left the room except Robert and his father and mentor, who worked out an action plan which Robert agreed to follow. This is a distinctive feature of the New Zealand model, considered to empower the offender and his or her family to resolve their own situation rather than be told what to do by social workers. Usually a larger number of members of the extended family are present, and often some of them offer to help to make sure that the action plan is followed. (4) The meeting then re-convened to approve the plan. Robert made an apology to Laura and her mother, which they accepted. He assured Laura that she would be safe in his company. He undertook to return to school, and the education worker undertook to assist in persuading the school to re-accept him. Robert's father asked about what help was available for Laura in putting the incident behind her; Laura herself felt able to continue her friendship with Robert's sister, which had been under great pressure. (*summarised from Mediation UK*, 2003)

There are different ways of conducting conferences, which have their advantages and disadvantages. In one version, developed in Australia, and now used in the Thames Valley Police area in England, the facilitator uses a questionnaire (script). Everyone stays in the room the whole time, and the proceedings end with refreshments to symbolise the reconciliation that has taken place. In another model (FGC), after the victim has expressed feelings and asked questions, a social worker will explain the options for reparation and for treatment available locally. Then everyone except the offender and his or her family leaves the room. During this private time with no one else present, they can work out a plan together, which they then propose to the victim, police officer and social worker.

Participation of victims is not as high as could be wished (Newburn et al., 2001), and some doubts have been expressed about whether the holders of official positions, such as police or judges, will be perceived as impartial mediators.

Sentencing circles

It is almost as if sentencing circles were a logical development of family group conferences. They similarly include families and supporters, but also other members of the community affected by the crime (such as shopkeepers if a shop has been robbed) or with a contribution to make (such as alcohol counsellors if alcohol is a factor in the offender's behaviour), and a judge, prosecutor and defence lawyer. They were introduced on the other side of the world, in Canada. They too are based on the traditions of indigenous people, and are also used with people from the majority population. Sentencing circles are not known to have been used in Europe so far, and to do so would probably require a change in the law in most countries. In Canada they are within the discretionary powers of the judge.

The circle includes a judge, is part of normal court proceedings and is subject to normal legal safeguards (among others: proceedings are open to the public and a record is made, the offender must participate voluntarily, the decision is subject to appeal). The circle does not make a proposal to the court – it is the court. There is therefore no limit to the seriousness of the cases that can be dealt with (except when the offence is so serious that a long prison sentence is necessary to protect the public or denounce the offence). Hearings last from two to eight hours, so it would not be practicable to use them for petty offences. Discussions go beyond the current offence to include preventive considerations: what had life in the community been like, what can be done in the community to prevent this dysfunctional behaviour, and who will support the offender and victim in ensuring that the sentence plan is successfully carried out.

The dominance of professionals is reduced, and that of community members is increased; care must be taken, however, to ensure that dominant members of a family or community do not exercise undue influence (see p. 28). But as a problem-solving approach to crime within a conventional justice system circle sentencing has many interesting features.[1]

Despite their variations, the methods used in the restorative processes described above have certain elements in common. These include:
- ground rules: the parties are usually asked at the beginning of a meeting to agree to basic ground rules, such as not interrupting, treating each other with respect, not using language that could cause offence. Also, mediators or parties may ask for a pause and parties may leave if they wish.

---

1. This account is summarised from an article by Heino Lilles, 2001, Chief Judge of the Territorial Court in the Yukon, Canada.

- active listening: mediators are trained in ways to encourage people to speak, such as body language, asking open-ended questions, and summarising not only the facts described but often also acknowledging the feelings.

- exploring options: people are encouraged to take responsibility themselves. Social workers or other officers may provide information about what is available, such as forms of community service, or training that the offender might need in order to find a job. But the parties themselves are encouraged to decide what is appropriate.

- informal confirmation: some mediation services provide refreshments at the close of a session, as mentioned above. They regard this not as an extra, but as an integral part of the process, in which both parties can relate to each other quite differently from the way they felt about each other at the beginning.

- confidentiality: mediators undertake not to reveal the content of the discussion, apart from the agreement (if any), and ask the parties to do likewise (although this cannot be enforced). The only exception is that mediators are bound by laws and/or professional standards requiring certain things to be reported, such as the imminent commission of a serious crime. Police officers acting as mediators may feel obliged to interpret this requirement more strictly. In particular, where information is disclosed in mediation that suggests that a vulnerable person, such as a child or a person with mental illness or learning difficulties, has been or may be the subject of abuse, it is important that practitioners are clear about the legal and professional requirements in their country for setting aside confidentiality and referring the case to the relevant welfare and protection agency. The parties should be made aware of this (see also 2.a).

The restorative process and the sequence of elements outlined are guided by two overarching working principles, namely empowerment and recognition.

Empowerment is related to mediation's essential element of participation. It starts from the premise that full participation in the process of mediation requires the capacity of both victim and offender to stand up for themselves and their interests, to speak out and to be able to agree on some things and disagree on others. Where these capacities are lacking completely, mediation must not take place. Where they are impaired on one side, it is the task of the mediator/facilitator to help the "weaker" party towards a more firm perception and articulation of his or her standpoint and interests. This kind of compensatory empowerment is a prerequisite of the mediation process, and it is the most important means for achieving the application of the working principle of recognition.

The concept of recognition pertains to interaction – or, more precisely, to the act of recognising the other person, or understanding his or her words and actions. In the course of restorative justice, the first act of recognition is that of the mediator, whose task is to "take in" each of the parties involved, and by setting this example, initiate the process of mutual recognition. This has to do with respect and understanding, but it delves too deeply to be explained by these two concepts alone.

The experience of "recognising the other" and "being recognised by the other" is part of the psychological development essential to mediation. Recognition is a kind of reciprocal interaction process that, if successful, enables one to overcome the opposing forces, or societal dynamics of domination and submission. True recognition can come only from one who has been recognised. Mutual recognition allows each party to withstand the tension of recognising the other as different while holding on to their own difference. Although these processes are complex, and can run the course of a lifetime, it is possible to catch a glimpse of their dynamics during mediation.

In this process, the mediator "recognises" both parties – accepting them and extending understanding. The effect should be twofold: each party gains recognition – first from the mediator, and is then better prepared to confer recognition upon the other. This enables both parties to hold their ground, while accepting that the other has different interests. This is done without submitting to or overpowering the other, by means of physical or psychological violence.

The reciprocity of recognition opens the pathway to feelings of remorse on the side of the perpetrator, and to forgiveness on the side of the victim. We must be aware however that the deep-reaching processes involved will not always occur, and that it may be wrong, even counter-productive, to apply pressure on the offender or the victim to try to make this come about. But when successful, these meetings are a powerful way of helping victims give an individual face to the offender. This can change their perception of the crime which has been committed and help them recover from it. For offenders, when they feel they have been recognised, their (often negative) self-image can be corrected, and they can feel less pushed into a defensive (minimalising or rationalising) attitude.

f. The need for an ethical framework

An ethical framework has a number of elements. First, there is a statement of values based on clarifications and justifications derived from ethical theory; second, there are principles derived from the statement of values; and, third, codes of practice derived from the principles (Mackay, 2000).

Growth of restorative justice as a movement and global demand for the implementation of restorative practices have created a "boom" market atmosphere. Everyone in the policy communities of our member states has heard of restorative justice; many want to try it out. However, it has perhaps been assumed that because it appears so simple, restorative justice is compatible with a wide range of political values and positions. This represents a serious risk for the future of restorative justice.

The apparent simplicity of the concept masks both the far-reaching nature of its potential impact on our understanding of the legal system, and the complexity of the task of implementing it in practice. It is apparent now that restorative justice not only represents a credible successor to the exhausted rehabilitative and retributive models, but that it is also emerging as a potential new theory of law (Mackay, 2000).

The rapid development of restorative practices has occurred in a dynamic political context. This is shown by the prominence in the media and political discourse of concerns about social control, presented under slogans such as "law and order", "social disorder", "anti-social behaviour", "war on crime" and the like. Restorative practices are propagated alongside measures such as electronic monitoring, increased use of custody and tighter social surveillance. This dual-tracking or bifurcation of penal policy creates serious strain for those who wish to develop restorative justice with integrity. There is a fear that restorative practices will become subsumed in policies that are primarily punitive in ethos and intention and that it will simply be seen as a set of techniques in a toolkit containing measures which are inconsistent with the values and principles of restorative justice. This context gives urgency to the view that restorative practitioners need ethical support and guidance in the highly contentious world of penal practices.

However, it is also true that restorative justice has acquired powerful juridical standing through the endorsement of the Council of Europe and the United Nations. Both these bodies have a strong allegiance to the concept of human rights. This suggests that restorative justice must develop its justifications, principles and practice codes within the over-arching concept of human rights. That is the most powerful ideological resource for an ethical approach to practice (Mackay, 1996).

The debates about whether restorative justice is the best model for responding to crime, or whether it can provide a theoretical underpinning for contemporary law, or how it can preserve itself in a policy context, are ones that are conducted in ethical terms. Whenever we refer to concepts such as "rights", "conflict resolution", "reparation" or "reconciliation", we are using language which carries strong moral inflexions and implications. Our justifications draw upon moral theories which help us determine what is morally preferable by reference either to duties and rules, to the consequences of actions, and a vision of human flourishing. When we use moral language in the pursuit of social objectives, we must be clear not only about what we mean, but also about the methods we are using to advance the claims. It is important that the claims of restorative justice are coherent because their radical nature is likely to set off a strong reaction. We cannot avoid ethical justifications for our claims on behalf of restorative justice.

Restorative justice theorists have couched their arguments in a number of schools of ethical theory: for instance, utilitarian, discourse ethics, neo-Aristotelian ethics. Without engaging in debate about the merits or shortcomings of these approaches, it is clear that those who support restorative justice will draw implicitly or explicitly on one or other or more of these types of argument. However, it is not enough simply to justify restorative justice and then select any practice that seems good or related to the idea. One has to be clear that the ethical argument supports the particular practice.

Issues that arise in developing an ethical framework

A number of exercises have been undertaken to develop codes of ethics or statements of principle. Generally these have not attempted a thorough linkage between ethical theory and practical codes. However, there are two examples of exercises that have brought ethical issues into the open. These are the "Commentary on the draft values and principles of restorative justice in criminal matters" and "Restorative justice program guidelines" by the Canadian Conflict Resolution Network, Policy Review Panel on Restorative Justice,[1] and "Setting the standard", an account of the Restorative Justice Consortium (UK) working group on Principles of Restorative Justice.

The attempt to write standards brings out a number of issues and dilemmas. Although we may be able to agree with statements such as the "UN basic principles on the use of restorative justice programmes in criminal matters", the way we interpret them in local contexts will give rise to debate. Quite apart from the legal and due process issues that arise in implementing restorative justice, there are a number of others that have strong ethical implications. Here are some examples.

How far should participation in restorative justice processes be voluntary? There is a strong view that both victims and offenders should be able to make an informed choice on whether to take part. This is advanced on the grounds that this most clearly conforms to the ideals of restorative justice, and because it is suggested that only if participation is voluntary will mediation be successful. However, it is also argued that if somebody has harmed another they have an obligation to make amends, and that society should enforce this.

What is the place of forgiveness? Some suggest that forgiveness is the best way by which the victims can be freed of the harm that has been done to them. There is thus a sense of pressure to participate and to forgive, particularly if the victim has a religious background. However, it is also argued that this is an unfair expectation of victims, and that restorative justice should go no further than to offer them a process which does not make forgiveness more difficult.

Parity of outcome. Even if non-participation in mediation does not lead to a more severe outcome than what would normally be expected, there is a problem if the outcome for one offender is different to that of another because one victim decided to participate and the other did not. (The same is true for victims in respect of the participation of offenders.) This is an issue of distributive justice.

Proportionality. Akin to parity is the issue of proportionality. Some have argued for a degree of proportionality between the offence and the form of amends, tempered by the capacity of the offender. Others have argued that this consideration merely replicates traditional legal thinking, which restorative justice should replace. It has been suggested that each victim and offender should be able to

---

[1]. See http://www.restorativejustice.ca and Restorative Justice Consortium, UK (1998) Standards for Restorative Justice, available at http://www.restorativejustice.org.uk.

agree on any amends which appear right to them, provided it is not excessive; but this still leaves "excessive" to be defined.

Punishment. It is a common assumption that restorative justice is inconsistent with punishment. This assumption is supported by arguments about minimal intervention. However, it is by no means self-evident that even if restorative justice were to be the pre-eminent theory of justice, that it would be able to abolish punishment.

Neutrality/impartiality. Although this appears to be an issue of due process, there is a profound issue of ethical integrity implicit in this topic. It has been suggested that persons implementing restorative justice should show respect to all individuals, while not condoning their actions (see 2.e below).

None of these issues can be resolved without recourse to debate involving a principled use of ethical and moral theory.

Conclusion

In order to have a workable ethical framework for a system of justice, we must engage in a cycle of practical reasoning that:

- identifies the ethical objective;
- questions whether existing practice fulfils that objective;
- attempts to reform or replace those practices that fail to meet our chosen ethical criteria;
- ensures ethical justification for new or reformed practice;
- clarifies the ethical components of language used in deliberations;
- provides principles for the implementation of new or reformed practices;
- provides codes of practice for practitioners;
- monitors the implementation of practice, and in particular compliance with codes;
- evaluates practice.

Such an ethical framework will enable us to assess and audit our own practice.

g. What can we learn from empirical research?

Restorative justice has been intensively researched during its short history; in some ways it has been subjected to closer examination than the conventional justice system. Of particular significance are meta-analyses which provide an overview of the evaluations of a number of programmes. This section will summarise two such reviews, and then present the findings of a selection of studies on specific issues.

A Canadian study (Latimer, Dowden and Muise, 2001) brought together twenty-two studies that examined the effectiveness of thirty-five individual restorative justice programmes, comprising victim-offender mediation as well as conferencing models. It included only studies that met a basic standard of research, namely those which used a control group, though not necessarily random assignment of cases to experimental and control groups. (The implications of this are discussed in section 5.a, under "Problems of designing evaluation research".) The meta-analysis showed that compared to traditional non-restorative approaches, restorative justice was more successful at achieving the outcome measures that were defined as its major goals. The results that were included and entered into the analysis were: victim satisfaction, offender satisfaction, fulfilment of restitution agreements and recidivism, when compared to more traditional criminal justice responses such as incarceration, probation, and court-ordered restitution.

One pronounced effect was victim satisfaction: victims who participated in restorative processes were significantly more satisfied than those participating in the traditional justice system. With regard to offender satisfaction, the differences – in favour of restorative processes – also proved statistically significant in every case except one. Unlike some studies (see below), the analysis showed slightly higher satisfaction rates (among victims as well as offenders) for victim-offender mediation programmes than for conferencing models. Quite positive outcomes were also shown with regard to the fulfilment of restitution agreements (but only eight studies could be included here).

Finally, the study showed that there is a low impact on recidivism. The authors argue that this is not surprising given the fact that restorative justice interventions are mostly limited to a short period of time. Restorative justice programmes should therefore be perceived as complementary to rehabilitative approaches; indeed it has been found that victims often regard the offender's co-operation with rehabilitative measures as a way of making reparation. If carefully designed and executed, rehabilitative programmes have a significant impact on recidivism.

The researchers concluded:

> Notwithstanding the issue of self-selection bias, the results of this meta-analysis, at present, represent the best indicator of the effectiveness of restorative justice practices, that is those individuals who choose to participate in restorative justice programs find the process satisfying, tend to display lower recidivism rates and are more likely to adhere to restitution agreements (Latimer, Dowden and Muise, 2001: 17).

Another meta-analysis of some twenty-five evaluative studies, encompassing forty-one restorative justice programmes in Anglo-Saxon countries, showed particularly positive results for conferencing programmes, in comparison with victim-offender mediation (McCold and Wachtel, 2002). Of all victims participating in a conference, 91% expressed satisfaction with the way their case was handled, and 96% expressed a sense of fairness. For victims participating in mediation, these figures were 82% and 85% respectively. Of all offenders participating in a conference, 95% expressed satisfaction, and 94% said they felt a sense of fairness. For offenders participating in mediation, these figures were 85% and 87% respectively. But even for mediation, victims and offenders on average rated these programmes as more satisfying and fair than traditional justice. An additional potential of the conferencing approach is that, through the active participation of community members, people surrounding the victim and the offender also benefit from the process.

Acceptance by the public

From criminological research in European and other countries, as well as from (international) crime victim surveys, we know that the general public is not as punitive as is often believed or claimed by policy makers or the judiciary (Weitekamp, 2000). Research in Germany demonstrated that judges and prosecutors can have more punitive attitudes than the general public (Sessar, 1992). Public attitudes depend, amongst other factors, on the degree and the kind of information the respondents have on the case and on the different options presented (Wright, 1989). If the process of victim-offender mediation is well explained, when people are confronted with having to consider concrete decisions about their fellow citizens, and have learned about victims' needs, people show strong support for this option. The general preference remains strong even when respondents have been victimised themselves in recent years. Knowledge of, and familiarity with, the whole approach of victim-offender mediation or conferencing clearly enhances public acceptance (Novack, Galaway and Hudson, 1980; Shapland, Wilmore and Duff, 1985; Umbreit, 1994; Lee, 1996; Ministry of Justice New Zealand, 1995).

Willingness of victims to participate

Sometimes doubts are expressed as to whether and why victims would agree to participate in restorative justice processes. Various studies show that 30% to 50% of all victims are interested in a personal meeting with the offender. This percentage increases up to 70% or more when the possibility for indirect (not face-to-face) mediation is also presented (Löschnig-Gspandl and Kilchling, 1997; Aertsen and Peters, 1998). From the victim's point of view, two motives for engaging in communication with the offender – direct or indirect – predominate: first, the need to receive more information and explanation about the offence and why it happened, and second, the need to convey a message to the offender, in order to make clear to him or her personally what the consequences of the offence were for the victim as well as for others. The need for financial compensation – although not negligible – is not usually the first concern that is mentioned. Comparing several studies, it has also been found that the way the mediation offer is formulated influences to a high degree the willingness of the victim to participate. Moreover, victims are more likely to feel able to participate in mediation if they have previously experienced a form of victim support (Reeves, 1989).

Degree of satisfaction

The degree of satisfaction with respect to the process and the results of mediation and conferencing in general has been found to be high for both victims and offenders in many studies (Umbreit and Coates, 2001; Braithwaite, 2002).

The empirical evidence from research indicates that victims in general show high levels of approval as a result of the restorative justice experience, even though the level is somewhat lower than for other participants in that process (Weitekamp, 2000). For offenders, levels of satisfaction with mediation or conferencing range between 80% and 95%, but victim satisfaction also goes up to 90% or even more in some studies. When participants in mediation are compared with victims and offenders who followed the normal legal procedure, the findings show, among other things, a decrease in victims' fear of re-victimisation by the same offender and fear of crime in general, as well as an increased satisfaction with the functioning of the criminal justice system as a whole (Umbreit, 1994). For conferencing, when cases were randomly assigned to a conference and to court, comparable findings were reported: after a conference a smaller proportion of victims show fear of re-victimisation, or feel anger towards their offenders, and many of them receive apologies, which seldom happens in court (Strang, 2002). It should be noted, however, that in some evaluative studies on family group conferences in New Zealand and Australia a minority of victims reported a negative experience.

The number of victims who participate in mediation programmes or conferences varies considerably. Victims might not wish to attend, particularly when they feel emotionally less involved (for example shop managers in the case of shoplifting). But victims have not always been invited to participate, a problem which can occur in more offender oriented programmes.

Questions related to victim and offender satisfaction were posed in the course of many of the research projects that evaluated specific (stand-alone) programmes, not only in the United Kingdom, but also in Austria, Belgium and Finland. Apart from the generally high satisfaction rates reported unanimously, studies that contained a wider range of differentiated questions and answers were also able to point out a programme's strengths and weaknesses and the influence of mediator performance. In the 1990s, a cross-national meta-evaluation study was carried out in four projects in the United States, later extended to include one in Canada and two in England (Umbreit, Coates and Roberts 1998). It used a quasi-experimental research design to compare experiences and perceptions of those who had been involved in victim-offender mediation (both direct and indirect mediation) with those who were referred to victim-offender mediation but who did not go through with it. Victims and offenders who participated in some form of victim-offender mediation in either of the two English projects were more likely to express satisfaction with the justice system's response to their case and to feel that the response had been fair, than those who were referred to the process but never participated in it.

Agreements reached and complied with

The number of agreements reached in victim-offender mediation and conferencing is high, usually between 70% and 90% of all cases started (Umbreit and Coates, 2001; McCold, 2003). More agreements are generated when there is a direct meeting between the victim and the offender (Hammerschick, Pelikan and Pilgram, 1994). The contents of the (usually written) agreement can be of a diverse nature: financial restitution, material reparation or a service to the victim, providing explanation for having committed the offence, apologies, or further commitments such as undertaking appropriate training or treatment.

The level of fulfilling the obligations agreed upon in mediation or conferences is very high as well, and substantially higher than for court orders to make reparation (Umbreit, 1994; Braithwaite, 2002). Compliance rates between 60% and 100% of the agreements reached have been reported, with the most frequently reported range between 80% and 90%.

The effect on re-offending

The type of evaluation usually receiving the most attention and especially from policy makers is the recidivism study. Since 1997, when elements of a restorative justice approach had become part of the mainstream response to juvenile delinquency in England and Wales, a more systematic and thorough evaluation effort was started. The government's approach, characterised as neo-correctionalism, emphasises control and prevention and accordingly we see a continuing preoccupation on the part of the British Home Office (as well as other governments) with reconviction rates as one of the key yardsticks by which to measure the effectiveness of restorative justice programmes (Dignan, 2004).

From several reviews of evaluative research, one can learn that no study so far shows an increase in the recidivism rate after victim-offender mediation or conferencing. A growing number of studies on victim-offender mediation and conferencing programmes demonstrate a modest, but positive effect on reducing re-offending (Umbreit and Coates, 2001; Braithwaite, 2002; McCold, 2003). However, many studies suffer from statistical weakness and other methodological shortcomings. Research progress has been made in recent years, which show a surge of positive recidivism results from the United States, Canada, Germany, the United Kingdom, Australia and New Zealand. The impact on reducing re-offending seems to be higher with serious rather than minor offences, personal rather than property offences, and offences with a direct victim involved. Equal participation in decision making and consensus on decisions are reported as factors that are related to lower rates of recidivism as well (Kurki, 2003). Braithwaite (2002: 95) found that "restorative justice can remove crime prevention from its marginal status in the criminal justice system, mainstreaming it into the enforcement process". His analysis draws on a broad study of restorative practices and on a value oriented criminological theory starting from informal, traditional ways of conflict handling and applied to both conventional and corporate crime.

A recidivism study has also been done in Austria; it was restricted to cases of minor assault by adult offenders and it used a control group of cases where for the same type of offence the court had imposed a fine (Schütz, 1999). The observation period was three years (after the case had come to the notice of the state prosecutor). There the conviction rate of the victim-offender mediation group was significantly lower than that of the control group: 14% for the victim-offender mediation cases as against 33% for the cases of offenders fined.

The quality of mediation

Some studies have been carried out on the quality of mediation and its effect on the outcome. Kathleen Daly (2003) has assessed the extent to which conferences live up to the claim that they treat victims and offenders with respect, evoke feelings of remorse in the offender, ensure that elements of the agreement are not excessive, and so on. She found that much is achieved, but there is a gap between the hope and the experience, and it may be easier to achieve some aims, such as fairness, than others, such as restorativeness itself. Maxwell and Morris (2001) in New Zealand have shown actual effects of the way in which a family group conference was conducted. Young people are less likely to offend again if they are not shamed and made to feel that they are "bad", and if they do feel involved in the decision making at the conference, and agree with the conference outcome. But many other factors in offenders' upbringing, such as problems in the family and at school, have an effect; these also have implications for crime reduction strategy. The research also shows the importance of what happens after the conference: social inclusion (having close friends since the conference) and gaining employment. In Thames Valley, in England, the accompanying research found that some police facilitators did make the offender feel like a "bad person"; some bad facilitation continued even after the researchers drew attention to it, and the hope that inappropriate police behaviour would be challenged in the conference setting was not always fulfilled (Young, 2001).

Financial costs

Studies of the financial cost of a victim-offender mediation case show considerable variations; from $97 in France (for the category of less time-consuming cases) to $250 in California and $1069 in Germany (Gimenez-Salinas, 1997; Umbreit and Coates, 2001). In Finland, it was calculated that the net cost saving of a mediation process in comparison to a court procedure was about €705 per case (Aaltonen, n.d.).[1]

One should take into account that financial costs or savings related to different options are difficult to compare. Normally savings will be higher when the programme is offered in an early stage of the criminal justice process. One can also expect that costs will decrease when a practice is implemented more widely. Mediation by volunteers rather than professionals may be expected to reduce costs, but the cost of supporting the volunteers adequately should not be overlooked. Finally, a discussion on the financial costs should be related to the aims and objectives of the programme, which can make clear that costs and benefits other than financial ones are important as well. Restorative justice could build "a social capital" through its effects on the community, by providing ways of active participation for victims, offenders, their supporters, community members and professionals (Kurki, 2003).

---

1. Some figures are given in US dollars because that was the currency used by the researchers. At the time of writing 1 US dollar was worth approximately 1 euro.

CHAPTER 2

PROMOTING AND IMPLEMENTING MEDIATION AND RESTORATIVE JUSTICE

a. Committee of Ministers Recommendation No. R (99) 19

The Council of Europe's Committee of Ministers Recommendation No. R (99) 19 concerning mediation in penal matters establishes important guidelines for the promotion and implementation of mediation. Drawn up by Committee of Experts on Mediation in Penal Matters, it was adopted in September 1999 (see appendix for the recommendation and its explanatory memorandum). Its aim was to bring together existing efforts in the field and assist the member states in setting-up or further developing mediation. It addresses the national governments of all of the member states, and since it was drafted in the framework of the European Committee on Crime Problems (CDCP), it addresses in particular their respective ministries of justice. The law and its institutions are at the centre of the recommendation. It consists of six main parts: "Definition", "General principles", "Legal basis", "The operation of criminal justice in relation to mediation", "The operation of mediation services", and "Continuing development of mediation".

The core sentence of the recommendation reads:

> The Committee of Ministers, under the terms of Article 15*b* of the Statute of the Council of Europe ... recommends that the governments of member states consider the principles set out in the appendix of this recommendation when developing mediation in penal matters ...

The principles[1] start with a definition of victim-offender mediation (quoted in part 1):

> ... any process whereby the victim and the offender are enabled, if they freely consent, to participate actively in the resolution of matters arising from the crime through the help of an impartial third party (mediator).

This definition relies on two main concepts: participation and restoration. From these concepts emerge the general principles laid out in the document. They are: the autonomy of mediation services within the criminal justice system; voluntariness, confidentiality and impartiality; general availability of mediation services and availability at all stages of the criminal justice process.

The autonomy of mediation services

Active participation of the parties involved calls for a certain autonomy of the mediation procedure. For this to be realised, mediation has to follow its own

---
1. These are found in the recommendation's appendix, which is considered the main part of the document.

rationale and design its specific inner structure as described above (section 1.e). This is different from the rationale characterising the criminal process. The latter is about the assessment of abstract guilt, the definition of the criminal act according to the penal code and the imposition of punishment or rehabilitation. Mediation, on the other hand, needs a setting that allows for open and unrestricted communication, the voicing of emotions and an active search for creative and practical solutions that respond to the victim's authentic needs and the alleged offender's actual capacity to "make good".

The kind of autonomy foreseen by the recommendation could be characterised as "conditional autonomy" within the criminal justice system. This status provides the time and leeway needed for the development of the open communication that allows mediation to unfold, and at the same time keeps the procedure inside the criminal law system. In this way, the state retains control of the reaction to a conflict (crime) that has come to the attention of the state prosecutor or has already gone to the judge, but the means of control are kept temporarily dormant. Victims and offenders are thereby enabled to participate actively and maintain their autonomy within the criminal justice system. During this interval the rationale of mediation and its internal rules govern the process. When everyone has had their say, and agreement is reached, the case is returned to the juridical logic, or rationale that was temporarily set aside, so that the prosecutor or judge can once more exercise discretion and choose to drop charges, prosecute or pass sentence.

Voluntariness, confidentiality and impartiality

The principle of voluntariness is derived from the concept of participation specific to mediation. Active participation – the argument runs – can be realised only if coercion is avoided. Voluntariness is a feature of any type of mediation. But doubts have been expressed about the lack of complete or "real" voluntariness with regard to the alleged offender (see chapter 1). Does not the impending penal procedure exert considerable pressure on the offender to "voluntarily" accept the alternative of mediation?[1] This topic has been dealt with extensively by the Committee of Experts on Mediation in Penal Matters and is closely related to the requirements of due process, meaning procedural safeguards (see section 2.b below). These legal safeguards protect parties from any undue pressure being exerted.

First, there should be no pressure from the outset to submit to mediation. Paragraph 11 of the recommendation's principles states this very clearly: "Neither the victim nor the offender should be induced by unfair means to accept mediation."

The recommendation's explanatory memorandum has further expanded on the topic of procedural rights and safeguards, based on Article 6 of the European Convention on Human Rights (ECHR), in particular, the right to a fair trial and to the relevant jurisdiction of the European Court of Human Rights in the "Deweer

---

1. In commercial and community mediation, there is also a range of pressures, including the possibility of litigation, that impels people to participate in mediation.

case".[1] This judgement deals with waiving the "right to a court" and the conditions under which such a waiver is compatible with procedural rights and safeguards of individuals in the criminal process, or in other words, whether the waiver was made under proper circumstances. Responsibility lies with the criminal justice authorities:

> They may not use any pressure against the parties in order to make them agree to mediation, and they should ensure that one party does not induce the other by threats and so on to agree to mediation.

This implies – with regard to the alleged offender – that the consequences of not having a mediation process (whether by choice of the offender or victim) should not be more severe than those ensuing from the mediation process, had it taken place.

Secondly, within the mediation session, there should be no pressure on the offender to offer too much reparation, nor on the victim to accept too little. The first safeguard against this can be the presence of supporters, especially in conferencing. The second could be providing an advocate, as is done in the New Zealand juvenile justice system, to advise but not represent the offender. There should also be access to legal advice for the victim (free if the victim cannot afford a lawyer's fees), but this is not yet available.

In relation to the intrinsic procedure of mediation, two features have received special attention in the recommendation, namely confidentiality and impartiality.

Confidentiality, or the rule that information exchanged during the sessions is to be kept between the participants, is an integral part of all mediation. The recommendation states this as a general principle: "Discussions in mediation are confidential and may not be used subsequently, except with the agreement of the parties". However, it was not easy to reach agreement on the exception to this principle. Paragraph 30 states that acquiring information on imminent serious crime in the course of mediation constitutes a reason, or even an obligation, to inform the appropriate authorities (often, but not exclusively so, the criminal justice agencies) and/or the persons concerned.

Even more controversial was the question – pertaining to mediation in relation to the criminal justice system – of to what extent the criminal justice authorities ought to be informed about what transpires inside mediation. The wording agreed implies protection of the principle of confidentiality insofar as it states that only the procedural steps and outcome of mediation are to be reported to the criminal justice authorities. "The mediator's report should not reveal the contents of mediation sessions, nor express any judgment on the parties' behaviour during mediation", reads the second sentence of paragraph 32.

Impartiality is of course mentioned as an important intrinsic quality of mediation. It is part of its definition and is set as a requirement in paragraph 26: "Mediation should be performed in an impartial manner …". However, mediation in criminal

---

1. European Court of Human Rights, Judgement of 27 February 1980, Series A, No 35.

matters is subject to special tensions. Naming and denouncing the act as wrong-doing is required. But at the same time the mediation procedure derives its strength from the capacity of the mediators to create an atmosphere where both parties are listened to attentively and both find "recognition", meaning understanding and acceptance as persons.

Mediation in criminal matters therefore has to absorb this tension and find a balance between naming and denouncing the (criminal) act beyond any doubt on one hand and on the other, reaching out to the alleged offender, and trying to restore the social bonds that have been severed. The explanatory memorandum states: "The requirement of impartiality does not imply that the mediator should be indifferent to the fact that the offence has been committed and the wrongdoing of the offender".

"General availability" and "availability at all stages"

These are stated as general principles, which provide a policy guideline for member states. After an initial pilot project phase, mediation should be made available throughout the country and at all stages of the judicial process. One has to be aware though that recommendations of the Council of Europe are generally not binding. In the realm of legal affairs they are intended to give orientation and support to legal policy arguments for those prepared and willing to use them. It needs the initiative of individuals, of groups, movements or institutions within the different member states to adopt in practice the intentions and the guidelines expressed in recommendations. The value and power of such recommendations are founded on the moral standing of the Council of Europe and the capacity of individuals and groups to use it in their promotion of the cause of restorative justice. However, for the recommendation to be effective, it must be translated into legal policies and legislation.

In summary, the recommendation provides clear guidelines that respond to most of the core issues that emerge in the course of establishing and promoting mediation services. However, it leaves the door open to an array of possible solutions and practical arrangements that can be used to fulfil the requirements of the principles laid out.

Follow-up on the recommendation

About two years after the recommendation came into force, the European Committee on Crime Problems commissioned a follow-up study to assess the degree and mode of the recommendation's implementation in different member states, and to determine the influence it had exerted.

The report was predominantly based on a questionnaire sent out to former members of the Committee of Experts on Mediation in Penal Matters and other experts, mainly associated with the European Forum for Victim-Offender Mediation and Restorative Justice, and on a seminar held as part of the second conference of the European forum (Ostend 2002). It led to the following findings.

By and large the recommendation had exerted a remarkable degree of influence in the member states. There are different paths that promoters of restorative justice can follow to initiate actions, drawing on the recommendation for support.

Users and promoters can be individuals who stand in close relationship to the government and/or are representatives of criminal law professionals, for example state prosecutors. Belgium, Cyprus, Finland, Italy, Slovenia, and to some extent Poland, provide ample evidence of this type of influence. There, the commitment of individuals dedicated to the cause of mediation has played an important role. They are individuals with a certain organisational affiliation with either the relevant ministry (the case of Finland), or with one of the professional groups of the criminal justice system (the case of Cyprus or of Slovenia).

In Czech Republic and Poland, it was non-governmental organisations (NGOs) that challenged national criminal policy and it was again the recommendation that proved to be a viable instrument with which to press their point. Although the new paradigm contained in the recommendation is presented in a very pragmatic and "realistic" way, the example of these countries also illustrates the difficulties in making it understood and accepted by agencies of the criminal justice system and its representatives.

In another group of countries, Albania, Bulgaria and Russian Federation, it was almost exclusively NGOs advocating victim-offender mediation that drew on the recommendation. Its contents wielded some influence on the methods used to set-up victim-offender mediation programmes and on practice and training. But in the realm of criminal policy, these programmes remain marginalised.

The recommendation's influence as observed in Austria, France, Germany, United Kingdom, northern European countries and Spain, and considerably later in Ireland and Portugal is of a different nature. If any influence it discernable at all, it is just the "general spirit" of the recommendation that has "mingled" with more specific national developments that have taken place, in the last decades in Austria and Norway, and sometimes intensified during the last three to four years, as in Belgium, France, Spain, Sweden and the Netherlands.

The recommendation had a marked influence on the final draft of the "United Nations basic principles on the use of restorative justice programmes in criminal matters". This was the result of co-operation, deliberately sought and established, between the members of the Committee of Experts on Mediation in Penal Matters and the group of NGOs that prepared the UN basic principles on the use of restorative justice programmes in criminal matters.

One should also mention the European Forum for Victim-Offender Mediation and Restorative Justice, a network created to promote international exchange of information and develop effective restorative justice policies, services and legislation. It is clear that such a network will use an international/European document as one of its pivotal instruments for achieving these objectives.

b. The necessity of a legal framework and safeguards

Recommendation No. R (99) 19 clearly provides for the preservation of the achievements of positive criminal law, namely the protection of a person suspected or accused of an infringement of the law from undue restrictions of his or her rights and freedoms through state power. Heike Jung, scientific expert to the Committee of Experts on Mediation in Penal Matters, has stated:

> Mediation is about adding a new quality, and not about doing away with the achievements of the process of civilisation in the realm of law. Referring to elementary supranational due process categories implies that mediation is not meant to be tied into an intricate web of legal formalism. But it has got to abide by some basic human rights requirements, such as those which have been enshrined in the European Convention on Human Rights.

Why should we have a legal basis?

According to the recommendation, "legislation should facilitate mediation in penal matters" (paragraph 6). Two more paragraphs (7 and 8) relate directly to the legal basis. But, says the explanatory memorandum:

> ... with a view to avoiding over-regulating mediation and considering the various approaches to mediation in member states, the recommendation does not explicitly require that mediation programmes should be laid down in law. Legislation should, however, as a minimum rule, make mediation possible and even facilitate its use. ... Mediation is of a less formal character than criminal proceedings are, in order to allow for a more personal and comprehensive approach to conflict resolution. This cannot, and should not, be regulated in detail.

Victim-offender mediation and other restorative justice practices are often characterised by the informal nature of their procedures and organisation. Most of these programmes, at least in the initial phase of development, are not created formally by law, but have a strong grass-roots character. The growth of restorative justice can be seen as part of an evolution towards less formal ways of dealing with conflict in society and the search for new, intermediate structures between the citizen and public authorities. From its side, the criminal justice system provides more and more leeway for negotiation and different types of participation.

But when restorative justice programmes are developing in a given country, one feels the need for some regulation. This regulation does not necessarily take the form of a formal law. Mediation practice is also directed by decrees, ministerial circulars and – probably the most common method – by good practice standards drawn up by mediators and their organisations. Moreover, the formal regulation of mediation is not exclusively the realm of criminal law. Mediation programmes can also be regulated by administrative authorities and regional governments.

But since mediation concerns criminal offences, one should not neglect its relation to criminal law and criminal justice. This type of mediation – in a broad sense – is part of a criminal procedure. Therefore, victim-offender mediation and other restorative justice programmes should be recognised (and supervised) by official bodies. Before, during and after the process of mediation, legal protection and safeguards should be available.

The need for a legal framework for restorative justice programmes is supported by at least three types of argument. The first one is of a strictly legal nature. It argues for a legal basis to restorative justice because of the principle of legality, which is – to a varying degree – central in criminal law in most west European countries. When mediation is legally recognised and defined, public prosecutors and other professionals have the legal grounds to work with it. It can offer a legal basis for those countries where public prosecution services are not functioning according to the principle of "opportuneness".

A second and related, but more pragmatic, reason for legislation is that it can be an impetus for broader and more frequent use of mediation as an option. It also provides governments with a legal framework for financing or subsidising programmes (which might be operated by NGOs). Such development would mean that mediation programmes are no longer dependent on the goodwill of local prosecutors or judges. Through legislation, mediation could be offered on a more systematic basis in the subsequent phases of the criminal justice process. The law could even oblige the judiciary to give a reasoned opinion in cases where the decision maker refrains from applying this provision (Groenhuijsen, 2000). Seen from the perspective of the persons directly involved – victims and offenders – the law would give them a right or at least equal access to mediation.

A third argument for legislating on mediation concerns the need for legal protection. A law on mediation would provide for judicial control procedures to evaluate the mediation process and its outcome in the light of certain legal principles such as equality, proportionality and *non bis in idem* (no double jeopardy), to name a few. Predictability and certainty should be promoted by the law, as should procedural safeguards and specific individual rights, such as the presumption of innocence, the right to legal assistance, the right to complain and informed consent to mediation.

With respect to the need for legislation, the European Union Council Framework Decision of 15 March 2001 on the standing of victims in criminal proceedings should be mentioned. This regulation defines mediation in criminal cases as "the search, prior to or during criminal proceedings, for a negotiated solution between the victim and the author of the offence, mediated by a competent person" (article 1).

Article 10 stipulates that each member state of the European Union

> shall seek to promote mediation in criminal cases for offences which it considers appropriate for this sort of measure" [and] shall ensure that any agreement between the victim and the offender reached in the course of such mediation in criminal cases can be taken into account.

Article 17 stipulates that this should be implemented through "laws, regulations and administrative provisions by 22 March 2006".

Legal safeguards

Legal safeguards and legal protection concern, as mentioned above, the respect for general legal principles, the guarantee of specific procedural safeguards and the protection of (other) individual rights. Judicial authorities should play a central role in providing and controlling these legal safeguards. But lawyers have an important task in this respect as well. Mediators should acknowledge and be familiar with these necessary legal safeguards and should assist in their implementation through good mediation practice and close co-operation with lawyers and relevant judicial authorities.

The elementary safeguard of voluntariness for entering into mediation has already been dealt with in the previous section. Voluntariness implies, amongst other things, informed consent, the right to refuse the offer of mediation without any pressure, and the right to go to court.

What about the "admission of guilt"? According to the principle of presumption of innocence (Article 6.2 of the European Convention on Human Rights) no decision on guilt may be taken by the criminal justice authorities without proper court proceedings. How can this principle be reconciled with mediation, which presupposes recognition of the facts, but which mostly takes place at a pre-trial stage, before guilt can be established? Mediation indeed makes no sense when the main facts of the case are ignored. Hence referral of a case to mediation should be guided by the requirement that the alleged offender admits a degree of responsibility for the act in question. According to paragraph 14 of the recommendation:

> The basic facts of a case should normally be acknowledged by both parties as a basis for mediation. Participation in mediation should not be used as evidence or admission of guilt in subsequent legal proceedings.

Thus, the alleged offender does not need to accept guilt in its legal definition. Furthermore, participation in mediation should not be used against the accused if the case is referred back to the criminal justice authorities after mediation. This makes it clear that the practice of mediation and restorative justice in general does not start from a legal conception of guilt, but from a broader, moral one. A more flexible and open definition is sought after, one that falls short of recognising criminal liability. Reference can be made here, for example, to the Austrian Juvenile Justice Act, which states that the offender has to "stand up or take on responsibility for his/her offence". Interesting in this regard is the Austrian legal provision that an act can cease to be criminal in nature because of later restorative actions performed by the perpetrator (Groenhuijsen, 2000).

Additional legal safeguards have to be implemented within the mediation procedure. The right of legal assistance, to translation and interpretation and – for minors – to parental assistance are explicitly mentioned by the recommendation (paragraph 8). These rights should apply during a mediation process. This implies that parties have a formal right during mediation to assistance from a translator if language problems emerge, or to support by a parent or another representative, in the case of juveniles.

What is less clear is whether the mediation process is helped by parties having access to a lawyer. Good practice in mediation recommends that parties should have the right to legal advice *before and after* the mediation session. But the presence of a lawyer *during* the mediation session is in general not seen as appropriate, unless the lawyer merely acts as an observer. Experience shows that the intervention of a lawyer during mediation can hinder the communication process.

Other legal safeguards should be provided for by the criminal justice system on the way it operates before or after mediation. When referring a case to mediation, a reasonable time limit should be established. After mediation is concluded, the principle of *ne bis in idem* comes into play. Paragraph 17 of the recommendation states:

> Discharges based on mediation agreements should have the same status as judicial decisions or judgements and should preclude prosecution in respect of the same facts.

This means that a dismissal, discontinuation or discharge after a successful mediation should be carried out formally, and be legally-binding – not just an informal practice by the public prosecutor or another authority. When no agreement is reached or when the agreement has not been complied with, and the case is referred back to the criminal justice authorities, then the decision on how to proceed "should be taken without delay" (paragraph 18 of the recommendation).

Types of legislation

By now, a growing number of European countries have legislated on victim-offender mediation. This legal framework can in some cases be applied to conferencing as well. Before presenting a general picture, we should comment that "mediation" is not always named as such in the law. In some countries, the law refers to mediation in an indirect way, for example when mentioning the possibility of restitution, conciliation or "taking responsibility" towards the victim. Further, when mediation is mentioned explicitly in the law the regulation is usually formulated in a very general way. This also implies that legal safeguards are not found in formal law, but – if at all – in subsidiary regulations, or are formed by jurisprudence. Moreover, formal law often contains no information on the position and organisation of mediation services or on the status of mediators. In general, three prototypes of legal regulation on mediation can be distinguished in Europe.

First, mediation can be provided for in juvenile justice acts. This is the case in Catalonia (Spain), England and Wales, Finland, Germany, Ireland and Poland. Mediation is in this case initiated by the public prosecutor or the judge (or in England and Wales, by the police or the probation service) and functions as a method of diversion.

Second, mediation, with respect to adult offenders, can be governed by a provision in the codes of criminal procedure (Austria, Belgium, Finland, France, Germany, Poland, Slovenia) and/or via a provision in the criminal code (Finland, Germany, Poland). In Austria and France, the code of criminal procedure also provides for mediation for minors (*réparation* in France). The most prevalent system is mediation initiated by the public prosecutor who, in accordance with his or her discretionary power, can decide to refer a case to mediation and arrange for appropriate follow-up once the mediation process is over. This is often a form of conditional discharge. In Switzerland, the possibility of mediation in a post-sentence stage, namely during a prison sentence, is foreseen by the criminal code, and supported by a federal law on victim assistance.

Third, mediation can be governed by an autonomous "mediation law", which determines the organisation and process of mediation in more detail. Such a law has existed in Norway since 1991 (the Municipal Mediation Boards Act, applying to both juveniles and adults, and covering criminal and civil cases). More recently (2002), Sweden adopted a law on mediation, also to be implemented in co-operation with municipal services. The Czech Probation and Mediation Act (2001) which creates a framework for probation and mediation services for all of the country, could also fall into this category.

A balance needs to be found between enabling legislation which will provide for mediation without ordering it, give flexibility to providers of mediation services and leave the development of mediation to the commitment and energy of these services on the one hand, and on the other, mandatory legislation which imposes a duty on officials to act. Legislation on mediation should not be too detailed and how it should operate should be laid out in official guidelines as these are more easily amended in the light of experience than are formal laws. It is important that those who draft laws and guidelines consult practitioners and academics having a vast understanding of restorative justice, or national or international organisations, to avoid setting up requirements that would hinder restorative practices from operating smoothly.

c. Organisational models

The way restorative justice programmes are structured as local services is often unregulated by law, as discussed above. How they are organised is dependent upon the type of restorative justice to be practised, whether victim-offender mediation, conferencing or sentencing circles. Each type involves other actors and requires a specific organisational framework. It also depends on whether the target group is juvenile offenders or adults.

In the first case, the programme is often, but not necessarily, part of special youth care services, court assistance or welfare services. Furthermore, the stage of the criminal justice process at which mediation or conferencing takes place is a factor in its organisation. As described in chapter 1, mediation for small offences can take place outside of the criminal justice system, for example in neighbourhoods or in schools. Mediation can also be introduced as a diversionary model at the level of the police, the public prosecutor or the judge; this is the most common model in Europe. Finally, mediation can function as a complement to the criminal justice process: parallel to prosecution, after sentencing, or even in the context of prison.

There are serious risks involved if the organisation of mediation services is seen predominantly in relation to the criminal justice system – whatever be the stage of the judicial process in which mediation could take place. The first risk is the tendency to apply legal categories to the practice of mediation. An example of this can be observed in respect to selection criteria and procedures: often legal categories based on types of crimes are the most important reference for considering a case, whereas restorative practices should be primarily based on the needs of victims and offenders, and their local communities. The second risk, related to the first one, concerns the over-emphasis placed on the offender's position, which still forms the main focus of the justice system and which risks taking hold in restorative justice programmes. Both of these practices could bias the way restorative justice programmes are conceptualised from the beginning.

The next section of this guide analyses how restorative justice programmes relate to the community. The role of NGOs and other ways of involving the local community are discussed. Here, we would like to present a global picture of how in European countries mediation programmes are organised along a spectrum: services by and large can be located somewhere on a continuum according to whether they are more system-based or community-based. Their position on this spectrum tells us a lot about their organisational framework (and often their working principles).

At one end of the continuum, are mediation services, such as penal mediation in Belgium, which fall completely under the authority of the judicial structures, in this case the public prosecutor's office. In some parts of England and Ireland, restorative practices function within police services. In France, one speaks – for the majority of programmes – of a "delegation" of authority to the mediation services or the mediators.

Furthermore, mediation services that function under, or are closely linked to probation services enjoy a certain level of autonomy, depending upon the relation of the probation service to the courts in that country. Thus in Austria the probation services have a semi-independent status, while in other countries they are much more dependent upon the courts or the Ministry of Justice. Mediation can also be part of, or be financed by, the correctional service, which then brings it again closer to the criminal justice system. The latter is much less the case where mediation is organised by local administrative public services, as it is in Norway and or Finland, where municipal social services deal with mediation. At the other end of the continuum we find mediation organised by independent NGOs, in cooperation with, of course, the courts. This is the case for certain initiatives in which have been taken in Belgium, England, France, Germany, Ireland, Italy and Poland.

As one moves more toward the community end of the continuum, the services of volunteers come into play. It seems more difficult, but not impossible, for judicial bodies to entrust authority to external volunteer services over which there appears at first glance to be less control (see chapter 4). One disadvantage of a more community-based service is that the impact its mediation will have on the criminal justice decision-making process is less certain.

Relevant here is a distinction made in the United Kingdom (Marshall, 1996). On the one hand there are mediation services working according to a "social work" model and on the other, according to an "independent mediation" model.

Mediation organised under probation belongs in the first category and is more offender-oriented. In this case, mediation is considered a form of social casework, mainly in an attempt to influence the offender's behaviour by confronting him or her with the consequences of the offence on the victim. In this model, mediation is limited to diversionary or post-sentence cases. Professionals play a dominant role and a directive mediation style is often used.

In the independent model, mediation provides more of an equal service to both victim and offender, and assists both parties in finding a common ground on which to work out their own solutions. There are few limits on the types of crimes or stages in this process. There is more leeway for using volunteers and the mediator acts more as a facilitator than as a third party actively directing the process.

In Germany, some mediators work directly for the judiciary. Not only does this give them less flexibility in the practical organisation of the service, mediation usually takes place in a court building, which is often regarded as less satisfactory for mediation, because then some victims perceive the service as being more offender oriented. The neutrality or impartiality of the mediation process should be reflected in the way services are organised.

The diversity in the way victim-offender mediation services in European countries are organised and positioned, should not necessarily be seen as a problem, as long as the elementary principles of good restorative justice practice are respected. Differences in the historical, legal, social, cultural and political context of European countries are responsible for this divergence. Neither should one underestimate the possible impact of particular events in society or in politics, which, for example, at a given moment draw all attention to the position of the victim or to the need for a better management of all types of community sanctions. This diversity shows, for example, how in some countries, such as Austria, Germany, Czech Republic and in England and Wales, probation services have taken the lead in developing mediation services. In other countries, such as France and Belgium, the victim perspective has been more at the forefront, although victim services in these countries initially had reservations about victim-offender mediation. Nordic countries have gone their own way and developed a more autonomous organisational model, where, as already mentioned, local municipalities – which in these countries are responsible for social services in general – host or support the mediation services. In Catalonia, the mediation service is part of the Department of Justice, whereas in Poland, formal guidelines do not allow persons professionally engaged in the criminal justice system to act as mediators.

Lastly, in federal states there is usually a division of competencies, which is highly relevant to how mediation services are organised. The federal level is responsible for issuing laws and other general regulations, while the regions or *Länder*, in the case of Austria and Germany, deal with financing and the practical organisation of the services. In some countries, this situation seems to hinder a sustainable and harmonious development of mediation services and practice. In other countries, this division of roles is seen more as a unique opportunity for making various sectors in society aware of their role in justice issues.

d. Mediation and the community

The criminal justice system rests partly on the idea that it would be burdensome for victims to prosecute offenders themselves, and on the pessimistic notion that if justice were left to the community it would be vengeful and violent. Restorative justice starts from the more positive belief that victims are largely concerned with reparation rather than revenge, and that the community is made up of many citizens of good will, who are willing to help repair the harm caused by crime. As we saw earlier, Nils Christie, in Norway, has famously argued that professionals have "stolen" conflicts from the people who really own them (Christie, 1977). For many years organisations and individuals have worked to reintegrate offenders into the community, and more recently to assist victims of crime as well. This fulfils part of the restorative aim, and will continue to be necessary for victims whose offenders are not known, and offenders whose victims do not wish to take part in mediation; indeed even when mediation takes place, further help is often needed, as will be seen below.

Community involvement can be considered at two levels: organisations and individuals. Restorative justice can be provided by independent organisations (NGOs, voluntary organisations, *freie Träger, associations sans but lucratif*), which may be managed by a board of local citizens, often including some professionals. Their aim is to provide a mediation service; this is clear, and does not conflict with the aims of the criminal justice system, as can happen if mediation is operated by the police or probation services. A local NGO can belong to a national umbrella body which may provide training and a system of accreditation to ensure high standards. It has been found that when mediation services are subsumed within a criminal justice agency, they obtain far fewer cases, probably because the selection and referral of appropriate cases is regarded as a subsidiary task by officers whose main responsibilities are elsewhere (Weitekamp, 2001). It has also been argued, however, that the stand-alone NGO risks being marginalised by the criminal justice system (Dignan and Marsh, 2001). Certainly NGOs need to be assured of adequate funding and close links with the system.

Both statutory agencies and NGOs can use volunteers as mediators, but NGOs are more likely to do so (see section 4.a).

Individuals, such as victims, offenders and their families, are also members of the community; conferencing in particular draws on the knowledge and abilities of extended families to find solutions that will be relevant to a particular offender, and often help implement them. An uncle or grandparent may, for example, have influence on an offender's attitude, or invite him or her to spend time at their home. At best, this can provide support and supervision of which neither the nuclear family (often a single parent) nor a social worker may be capable.

Community involvement cannot however be limited to the mediation process itself. Victims who find it stressful may need support, and the minority who find it painful (Strang, 2002) must not be forgotten. Offenders who are willing to make reparation must be enabled to do so. Suitable placements for reparative community work have to be found, perhaps with social services or NGOs, and many offenders have basic needs linked to reintegration: employers who will provide work, suitable accommodation, and so on. Training in literacy, social and vocational skills and parenting, as well as treatment for drug addiction and so on need to be provided by NGOs or by the community collectively, as represented by the elected local authority. There are also programmes to meet special needs, for example, mentoring, in which a stable, trained person guides a vulnerable one who lacks a supportive role model, and circles of support, in which a group of trained volunteers works with sex offenders – usually after their release from prison. The latter is being pioneered in England, using a Canadian model. Any evaluation of restorative justice, especially in relation to re-offending, should examine the adequacy of these support services as well as of the mediation or conferencing process itself.

Above all, the community has a vital part to play in crime reduction. First it has to devote adequate resources to dealing with pressures identified as likely to lead to crime; an example of this would be the Sure Start programme in the United Kingdom, which offers support to inexperienced and vulnerable parents of children under five.

Mediation and conferencing can also contribute. The non-adversarial, informal atmosphere of the mediation session can encourage offenders to talk about the context in which they acted as they did. Mediators can collate this information, for example evidence of high unemployment, inadequate schools or vocational training, racial discrimination, lack of recreation facilities, and so on, and pass it to those responsible for crime reducing strategies.

Restorative justice consists of much more than a mediation session which lasts for perhaps one or two hours; it is part of a whole agreed "package" in which the offender's willingness to "make good" must be matched by the community's willingness to make this possible.

e. Training and education

Training mediators

"Mediation between people who have been divided by crime is one of the most skilled and sensitive tasks to which anyone could be assigned." (Marshall, 1999). Nevertheless, the quality and extent of training in Europe shows a very diversified picture, as clearly shown by a survey performed under the auspices of the European Forum for Victim-Offender Mediation and Restorative Justice. No agreed European minimum standards for training victim-offender mediators currently exist.

Mediating between victims of crime and offenders does not require only technical skills. Mediators must have a wide range of personal skills as well, which mediation services should use as selection criteria. These include:

- good communication skills, particularly listening;
- problem-solving and negotiation skills;
- a commitment to equal opportunities;
- the ability to feel empathy for different kinds of people;
- a good understanding of local cultures and communities;
- the ability to acknowledge, recognise and deal with personal preconceptions and prejudices;
- the ability to remain neutral and non-judgemental;
- the ability to handle strong and difficult emotions in others;
- patience;
- the ability to control the process while empowering the parties to take control of the content;
- mental agility;
- the ability to offer and receive constructive feedback;
- a commitment to learning and improving one's own mediation skills;
- the ability to work under supervision.

Recommendation No. R (99) 19 (paragraph 23) adds that mediators should be able to demonstrate sound judgement, which would normally be related to a high degree of maturity. Such skills are widely spread across the population and are by no means related to educational level. This means that mediators can, and should, be selected – as proposed in paragraph 22 of the recommendation – from all sections of society.

Training of mediators should consist of two broad, interlinked parts: knowledge, and understanding and skills.

As regards knowledge and understanding, trainees must be more than well-informed on restorative justice and mediation. Mediation requires a good knowledge of the criminal justice system, legal rights of participants and services linked to the criminal justice system. Often participants in mediation have questions about the criminal justice procedure and the way mediation will impact on this. If the mediator is not able to answer these questions, he or she should be able to refer the participants to the appropriate service. The mediator usually explains legal rights when the possibility to mediate is explored.

Basic training of mediators should include a good introduction to victimology in order to better deal with victims and their situation. Mediators should know how victims experience crime, the different phases they go through when coping with the effects of crime and victims' rights. Further, they should be able to detect signs that victims are not coping well with the aftermath of crime, and should know which services to refer them to for help. It is clear that even the offer of mediation, let alone actually meeting the offender, is very demanding for the victim. There is a risk of secondary victimisation. Therefore, a thorough knowledge of the way victims cope with the aftermath of an offence is crucial. It is best, in this respect, that for this part of the training, victim support services are asked to contribute. They will be the most adequate people to convey the different aspects of victimisation.

But a thorough knowledge of the "world of offenders" is also very important if the mediator is to cultivate empathy for the offender. One of the basic principles of restorative justice is that it is the criminal act that should be denounced and not the offender; the offender is not a "bad" person, but his or her acts were wrong. This is an important factor in the reintegration of the offender. Many come from an underprivileged background, and this has implications for what offenders can realistically do in terms of reparation towards the victim. Mediators should be aware of the services in the community that offenders can turn to in order to get help, such as debt counselling, treatment for drug addiction, and so forth.

In addition to knowledge, future mediators should be trained in a considerable variety of other skills, including how to:

- persuade parties to participate without putting pressure on them;
- maintain impartiality;
- deal with "difficult" people;
- deal with overt or covert hostility;
- handle conflict and the expression of emotions, particularly anger;
- identify obstacles to mediation;
- become aware of one's own prejudices.

Summing up all the skills that are needed for mediation would be too time-consuming to do here. However, it is important to be aware of the fact that bringing two parties in conflict together is not an easy ride. If one of the parties tries to dominate the session, the mediator must be able to re-establish a balance between them. Mediators must be able to intervene in an appropriate way when, in trying to reach agreement, one of the parties is making unrealistic demands, and to stop mediation when it becomes clear that it is too painful for the other.

During training sessions, mediators should continue to be assessed so that any concerns about their suitability to act as mediators can be taken into account.

Training must be interactive, participatory, and experiential, with a varied format that allows for different learning styles through the use of videos, written material, brief presentations, discussion, case histories, exercises, skills practice, and modelling of skills and processes. There is a consensus that role playing is essential in effective mediation training and that a lot of time should be spent practising skills in small groups. In some places, trainees will also have to go through an apprenticeship, during which they will work together with an experienced mediator.

The extent to which a mediator should be trained differs depending on the types of cases to be dealt with. Mediation for serious and violent crimes requires additional skills and knowledge compared to mediation for low-scale crimes that have a more limited impact. The duration of training is currently very diversified in Europe. An experienced trainer has suggested that 120 hours is needed to include important elements such as victimology, counselling among colleagues, learning in groups and dealing with one's own reactions to conflicts during training. In England, in contrast, community mediators will probably receive about 35 hours' training, plus some role plays, and will perform their first visits and mediations in the company of an experienced mediator.

However, the explanatory memorandum for Recommendation No. R (99) 19 states: "… their [mediators] training should continue throughout the course of their work". Indeed, continuing education should be built around issues in the field, advanced skills development (for example via case review) and needs expressed by mediators. Mediation services should make in-service training mandatory and a requirement for renewal of accreditation.

Currently, training is being offered by the mediation services themselves, by ministries of justice or by general education organisations in co-operation with mediation services. It is recommended that a national organisation should oversee all training initiatives in order to ensure high standards.

The quality of mediation work should be similar throughout Europe, and a Europe-wide effort should be made to draw-up a commonly agreed basic framework for the training of mediators.

Educating partners and the general public

To set up good co-operation with the criminal justice system, partners should have at least a basic knowledge of what mediation and restorative justice are. This is especially true for "gatekeepers", administrators, prosecutors, judges and anyone who makes important decisions about the handling of individual cases and the allocation of resources. Judges in particular should be informed well enough about it to act as one of the safeguards for participants. For example, when a case that has been to pre-court mediation comes before them, they should be able to ask the right questions to make sure that the mediation or conference has been as restorative as possible. Judges should ensure that the appropriate people were invited and that participants were satisfied with the process and the agreement reached. As will be seen later (section 3.c), criminal justice professionals sometimes have inaccurate preconceptions with regard to restorative justice. It is important to correct these misconceptions in order to create a good working relationship.

An introduction to restorative justice should be included in law school curricula and a more in-depth course should be part of all in-service training for the professions related to criminal justice (see also section 3.c).

Finally, the general public must also be informed about restorative justice. This will be dealt with in section 4.d.

CHAPTER 3

HOW TO SET UP MEDIATION AND RESTORATIVE JUSTICE PROGRAMMES

The process of establishing a mediation service will vary from country to country, but generally consists of three basic elements: assembling a group of people (a steering committee), developing a programme and making the necessary decisions, and implementing them. This will involve identifying the legal basis for mediation, particularly within the criminal procedure which makes it possible; acquiring sources of funds; and explaining the idea to professionals and the general public (see section 4.d). This chapter outlines the process of establishing a mediation service in an area (and possibly a country) where none has existed previously. At a later stage nationwide introduction of restorative justice, and possibly changes to the law, will need to be considered. The Council of Europe's Committee of Ministers Recommendation No. R (99) 19 provides a useful checklist of points on the subject.

a. Initiating a programme

Different preconditions prevailing in different countries have to be taken into consideration. The strategy to follow will depend on the structures of the public sector in relation to the non-governmental sector, meaning the relative strength and flexibility of government agencies on the one hand, and of non-governmental organisations (NGOs) on the other – and the way they relate to each other. And it also depends on traditions and attitudes. Whatever the strategy chosen, it will need to bring people together, and be used to develop and implement a programme.

Bringing people together – the steering committee and its composition

Usually there will be individuals, people active within an NGO or governmental or municipal agency, who will start the initiative. They will take up the issue of promoting the restorative mode of dealing with crime and its aftermath. In any case it needs at least a few representatives of the criminal justice system who are prepared to make referrals to the restorative justice service or to make provisions for restorative justice procedures within their realm of competence and discretion. It would be an advantage if these representatives had a good professional reputation to give their opinions sufficient weight. They will need to consider not only the advantages of restorative justice for victims and offenders, but its effect on their own work; as far as possible methods should be designed which will reduce their workload rather than increase it.

From the very beginning, victim support services (if they exist) should become involved and contribute their knowledge and experience. In short: any type of organisation with a stake and a policy interest in legal/criminal matters should be contacted by those instigating a restorative justice programme. It is important that stakeholders do not feel left out and consequently become wary of the initiative. In addition, a joint effort in itself is one of the strongest motivating forces.

Another important element is eliciting and promoting community involvement. As has been said earlier, the degree and the mode of community involvement depends on the overall socio-political structure of a society. In any case, it will be up to the steering committee to seek contact with existing community organisations and to elicit their interest and their active support. This may consist of electing lay people to the management committee of the mediation service, but it can also mean using trained lay people as mediators, either as volunteers or paid for each session that they facilitate. The use of volunteers will depend on local circumstances. In areas where incomes are low and many people may work long hours and/or hold down more than one paid job, there is little time (and perhaps no longstanding tradition) for voluntary work. This may indicate a need to pay mediators, as is done in some places in England, and in Poland, where cases can be referred to "trustworthy persons or organisations" (Article 320, section 1, Code of Criminal Procedure). Another example is Slovenia where, following the example of Norway, victim-offender mediation is done by mediators who receive remuneration for each case they handle.

The importance of having skilled mediators, if restorative justice is to be implemented well, cannot be exaggerated. The recruitment, training, support and supervision of mediators needs an effective organisation to provide for this, as well as adequate budgetary provisions. (see sections 2.e/3.b). Introductory seminars should also be organised so that judges, prosecutors and other criminal justice personnel can gain a better understanding of mediation, even though they will not have to practise it. At national level, an organisation should be set up to oversee training content and the competence of trainers.

A useful tool for motivating and activating an already existing initiative consists in inviting practitioners and academics from other countries who can provide first-hand-information from experience gained elsewhere. This strategy is promoted by the European Forum for Victim-Offender Mediation and Restorative Justice, and has been followed by most of the central and eastern European countries, including Poland, Slovenia, Czech Republic, Hungary and Russian Federation. It is important that these contacts include criminal justice professionals, especially public prosecutors, judges and police officers. Members of the same professions are often better able to "convince their colleagues" when explaining an innovative practice than academics and members of another, albeit neighbouring profession.

We are aware however that in the field of law and the legal professions the language barrier is difficult to overcome and special efforts will have to be made in that respect. Julex (available at http://www.ju-lex.com), a dictionary of legal terms, is a first step in this direction.

Strategies for designing and developing a programme

The steering committee will also have to decide the stage, or stages, of the criminal justice process at which cases can be referred to mediation. As was seen in chapter 1, the earlier a case is referred to mediation, the more time is saved by the criminal justice system. On the other hand, there exist severe restrictions as to the feasibility of referrals at different stages, dependent on the principles guiding the respective criminal justice systems. Police referrals are more difficult to arrange in a system where there is almost no margin for police discretion. Generally speaking, it would be a mistake to think that, when setting up a restorative justice model, one has a free choice from a spectrum of possible models. This choice is always a restricted one. Nevertheless it would be advisable to gain a thorough knowledge of existing models including their advantages and disadvantages (see section 2.c).

Restorative justice programmes can be defined and located within the parameters of a country's legal system, taking account of sociological factors and the availability of resources. At the initial stage, the steering group should design a programme that will function within existing law, and once a mediation service is established, proposed changes in the law can be made.

Before a mediation service can begin operations, some key decisions have to be made. Some of these concern how the service will fit in under the criminal justice system. This depends on the law and other factors in the country concerned, and will require negotiation and probably some public awareness-raising (see section 4.d). Will the mediation service operate as diversion from prosecution, as part of a sentence, after the sentence, or a combination of these? Other decisions relate to the model of mediation to be used: victim-offender mediation or family (community) conferencing, one mediator or two, with or without a "script" (written text for mediators to follow) and so on.

Victim-offender mediation is still the most well-known and the most easily accessible restorative justice model, especially in central and eastern European countries. It is, however, seriously worth considering family (or community) conferences. Although not yet widely used in Europe, they are being increasingly introduced, and appropriate conference models could be devised and set up.

There is not yet sufficient research evidence to determine the relative merits of one-to-one mediation as compared to that of conferencing or sentencing circles. The effort needed to set up family and community conferencing is such that strategically, this type of mediation is best used in cases of serious crime. In terms of cost efficiency, conferencing for petty crime would not be justified or appropriate. Evidence also shows that prevention of further crime is more likely to be an outcome in cases of more serious crime. (Sherman and Strang, 1997). Sentencing circles would hardly be feasible within inquisitorial jurisdiction, without some fundamental changes in criminal procedure as it stands now.

Participation

It is important to strive for maximum feasible victim participation within any type of restorative justice practice. In the case of conferencing, this implies a conference set-up that includes the victim and his or her supporters, and one which is not restricted to the offender's wider circle of family, friends, and supportive network. There is a tendency to focus more on the offender and rehabilitation and less on empowering victim and offender to resolve actively the conflict themselves. Attention must be given to the method and timing of contacting victims: ideally this should be done by trained mediators, or failing that by people with training in restorative justice.

With regard to participation, in cases where the victim is not an individual person or is not prepared to personally confront the offender, the presence of community representatives is valuable; their aim should be to present an authentic description of the victim's experience and feelings, but without moralising.

The types of case to be considered for referral will also have to be decided. As has been mentioned, most services aim to exclude the less serious offences, unless the victim is badly affected, and to include relatively serious ones as far as possible.

Setting-up pilot projects is generally the best way to end up with well-established and well-funded restorative justice services. Experience shows that when introducing a new and unusual way of dealing with a problem – in this case with the consequences and the aftermath of crime – nothing convinces more than actual practice. Pilot projects which are part of the criminal justice system are less problematic in common-law systems, where at each stage there is sufficient scope for exercising the principle of discretion (opportuneness). But in civil law countries where the principle of legality (mandatory prosecution) prevails, ways and means have been employed, usually provided by an article of existing legislation, that allow for the prosecution process to be disrupted under certain conditions. For example, under a previous version of the Austrian Juvenile Justice Act (JGG) it was article 12 that gave the state prosecutor power (except in more serious cases) to drop charges when the prognosis for no further offending was good. Directly compensating the victim, materially or otherwise, was perceived as supporting a positive prognosis.

But it should be pointed out that the Austrian pilot project led to serious debate as to whether pilot projects within the justice system are compatible with the principle of equality of treatment. Having a separate model, a special track for certain cases/offences that are brought before the criminal justice system, implies – at least while the pilot project is running – regional inequality within a country's jurisdiction. Can such a breach of the right to equal treatment before the law be justified? The answers were mainly affirmative, stating that temporary pilot projects serve the purpose of making the array of criminal law reactions more adequate and more effective (relevant contributions on this subject are available only in German: Bogensberger, 1994; Schüler-Springorum, 1991).

Another point of entry for victim-offender mediation, used by the public prosecutors in Italy, is the provision of a "personality assessment" or pre-sentence report within the criminal procedure applied to juvenile offenders. This procedure has been extended accordingly to allow prosecutors to refer cases to mediation services. In France, Article 41 of the Code of Criminal Procedure allows for this

(Jullion, 2000, p. 235). Finding legal provisions that can be used for the referral of cases within a civil-law system must not be confused with the skill of an individual lawyer who is "stretching" the law to serve his or her and the clients' interests. We recommend a common effort to seek out strategies that are compatible with existing law as a provisional arrangement for making case referrals.

Summarising these experiences and considerations shows that a suitable and feasible "place" needs to be found, within existing criminal law and the respective legal provisions, where pilot projects can be fitted in, until such time as the law can be amended.

As can be seen by examples from many countries (Austria, Belgium, Spain (Catalonia), Sweden, Finland), pilot projects have paved the way for (nation)wide expansion and for the introduction of new legislation. Provisional arrangements have been replaced or complemented by special legislation on one of the different types of mediation (section 2.b).

Whenever possible, pilot projects should be accompanied by research. We strongly recommend the model of accompanying research, combining evaluative research and action research. The accompanying research model differs somewhat from that of evaluative research, and has proved very helpful when researchers have an interactive relationship with practitioners. This should stimulate ongoing reflection and self-evaluation on the part of practitioners and provide them with theoretical and methodological tools that guide this reflection. An essential part of this kind of research is scientific evaluation, and its results are a starting point for further discussion and for ongoing development and improvement of a service. In addition, research and scientifically supported evidence can be used to underpin arguments for promoting and expanding the restorative justice practices tried out in the course of the pilot project.

Setting up a permanent restorative justice programme

When a pilot project has come to an end, and a report on its work and research has been finalised, the next step consists in making a case for the continuation and expansion of the project. Its work and research results need to be made known to the public, professionals and policy makers. The pilot project in itself is a process leading towards this goal, in the course of which the stakeholders should be involved or at least informed.

Extending the circle of interested groups and persons contributes to the setting-up of restorative justice practices on a wider scale. At this stage the question of funding arises once more – this time about continuing funding.

b. Acquiring funding

Funding restorative justice programmes may be considered from the point of view of an NGO or an agency within the criminal justice system applying for funds, or from that of an administrator, who decides whether funds should be granted.

Those seeking funds for restorative justice programmes have to ask the same basic questions as those with new ideas or projects to "sell":

- What are we seeking funding for?
- Who holds the funds we might attract?
- How does the project fit in with the funders' objectives?
- How can we persuade the funders to invest in restorative justice?
- What has been agreed with the funder?

Grant-givers in turn have to consider whether the money will be used as effectively as possible.

What is the funding for?

As indicated in the last section, funding might be sought either for an initial pilot project, or on a more mainstream (long-term) basis. However, these are ideal models. In practice, other contingencies come into play. Pilot projects may require extension because evaluations have not been completed. Funders may give grants or offer contracts for limited periods only. Some funders may require the participation of other funders, which can be positive as it gives the programme a degree of independence from the policy priorities of a single grant-giving organisation.

Funding may be required for a national NGO supporting and promoting restorative justice, or for a restorative justice service directly. In either case, a project needs to be clear about its aims, objectives and activities and how the proposed activities fit in with the relevant legal and policy context of the jurisdiction under which it is operating. It is to be hoped that later this context will itself become more restorative.

Budgets must be realistic in order to provide for an adequate infrastructure (rental of suitable premises, interior furnishing, heating systems, communications systems and so on) as well as proper levels of staffing (scales of remuneration, training, books and professional journals, membership in relevant organisations, travel and subsistence), and for obligations pertaining to different types of insurance (health insurance, travel, etc.) Finally, one must distinguish between requests for capital and revenue funding.

It is worth asking potential funders what degree of flexibility they are willing to permit in the movement of funds between budget headings. This is important, because sometimes, particularly at the initial stages of a project's life, actual expenditure may vary significantly from what was forecast. This can result from various causes, such as a slow start in receiving referrals or recruitment difficulties.

Who holds the funds which the programme might attract?

Depending on the historical and political context of individual states or regions funding may be available for new initiatives or to sustain new practices. State funds may also be available at national, regional or local level, or even internationally, for example through the European Commission. Funds may also come from public donors (national or local government or government agencies), and private sources such as charitable or philanthropic trusts and commercial companies or even private individuals (donors). Private sources often define the areas to which they will contribute, locally, nationally or internationally.

It is important to undertake effective reconnaissance work on potential donors, for example to single out the key decision makers and the "gatekeepers" to the funding process, and if possible to establish a personal rapport between potential funders and project actors.

Larger trusts often have information packs or websites explaining the type of work they support, which include their application form, and the dates of their meetings. Sometimes an officer from a government agency or a trust fund will give advice on the best way to present a programme, which is a good way of avoiding wasting everybody's time with an inappropriate application.

Some funders will be partners in service delivery. These will be local authorities or representatives of central government who will be responsible, either themselves or in partnership with other agencies – such as public prosecutors or courts, for making referrals as well as providing funds. Other funders (donors) do not usually get involved in the actual operation of the project. However, if the work is of a promotional nature, it is possible that the donor will also participate in partnership work, as one national charity in the United Kingdom has done in the past.

How does the project fit in with funders' objectives?

It is important to have a clear picture of the agendas, expectations and policies of potential funders. Sometimes they can be influenced to adopt wholly new objectives, but one is more likely to persuade them to support a proposal if it is presented as a novel way of carrying out their objectives, and as consistent with their own existing policies and remit.

Governmental organisations will need to work within current political agendas, which may include items on reducing offending, fear of crime, inefficiency and dysfunctions of the current criminal justice and penal systems. It can also be argued that restorative justice measures are likely to have other politically useful results such as improvements in schools, community-building and reconciliation.

With private sources, there is more scope to present some of the more idealistic elements of the restorative justice agenda, such as the potential for peace-making or individual healing.

It has to be recognised that we are "selling" restorative justice in a market place where the different aspects of restorative justice are seen as desirable commodities. And it is our task to demonstrate that restorative justice is better than retributive or rehabilitative models. The restorative justice model does not simply replace other models, it provides added value. To put it more crudely, funders get back more than what they put in. And in the case of money allocated from the state, taxpayers also reap the benefits.

Nor does this entail selling restorative justice simply as a commodity to raise funds, and having to adapt our principles accordingly. Only limited compromises should be made to meet the conditions of funders (donors) as purchasers. The basic model of restorative justice must remain intact, otherwise it will no longer be restorative. This may mean "declining to do business" if the purchaser will undermine public perception of the "brand" through misuse of the product, for example by presenting restorative justice as if it were a punitive response to crime.

What do funders require from an investment in restorative justice?

Funders have to be satisfied that the project is sound. The project team must first show potential funders that it can handle funds appropriately, and persuade them that restorative justice is an attractive idea that is feasible. The intuitive appeal of restorative justice must be developed. However, potential funders also require good reasons to back their initial attraction to the concept.

A programme can achieve this by demonstrating the success of restorative justice, through relevant research studies. However, there is also room for debate between the applicants and the funder or donor. Grant-givers will not be impressed by exaggerated and unfounded claims for restorative justice, but they will want to be assured that the principles and practice of restorative justice deal effectively with the potential difficulties of implementing the model in any particular jurisdiction. The also want to be assured that it will fulfil their existing objectives in a better way.

Above all, we should attempt to engage with public opinion in order to influence the political and public media-communications culture that restorative justice is a good thing (see section 4.d). Supporters of restorative justice need to develop effective communication strategies for a variety of audiences. Feedback from communication activities (surveys, focus groups, and so on) can make a big difference to the receptivity of funders.

After persuading potential funders that restorative justice is a good model, the next objective is to demonstrate that a particular proposal is workable and that it has the support of future partners in the project. In the case of continuing funding, it should be shown that the initial pilot has met and preferably exceeded expectations; this is another reason why research is important. In either case, it must be clear how the project will operate, what results are expected and how the project will be evaluated.

Another and often forgotten objective is to persuade the funder that the project is the type of organisation with which they can work confidently and efficiently. How does one do this?

The most important factor here is to present the organisation as competent in its way of doing business. The organisation must be well-structured and well-run. It must conform to the best standards of governance for NGOs or public services, and have a clear vision and mission.

It should be constituted effectively either as a partnership of statutory organisations, or as an NGO. In the latter case, this means having the appropriate legal constitution as an NGO, or not-for-profit limited company (or equivalent in each jurisdiction) in order to limit the liability of members of the board of management. The organisation may need to be constituted as a not-for-profit NGO or charity in order to be a recipient of charitable donations from some donors.

Members of the board of management should be fully aware of their legal responsibilities, specifically their fiduciary responsibilities as trustees of public or charitable funds, of laws relating to insolvency and the limits of protection from incurring penalties as a result of negligent handling of the organisation's finances. As a matter of caution, they should make sure that they have adequate insurance policies to cover their potential liabilities, especially those prescribed by law.

Grant-givers will want to be assured that the organisation has effective management structures, including those for:

- financial control;
- health and safety;
- quality development;
- audit and evaluation of work;
- human resource management;
- upholding human rights principles at the workplace;
- staff training and development; and
- operational management of staff.

It may be possible for small organisations to obtain guidance from public advice bodies, or sympathetic professionals.

It is also important to ensure that a board of management has the requisite management skills to record and communicate the decisions of the board, oversee the development of policies, and manage finances. Recruitment of a treasurer can pose problems. It may be useful to search specifically for someone with specialised financial expertise, and also for someone with experience in fund-raising; these two roles may require people with different sets of skills. Board members cannot be paid for their services if the organisation is a not-for-profit one.

What has been agreed with the funder?

It is in everyone's interest to be clear about the funder's expectations. A document should be drawn up specifying amongst other things, the nature and content of the service, its criteria for referral, its expected outcomes (including expected through-put of work, and its projected impact on the service users), and methods of monitoring, follow-up of cases, and evaluation.

There should be mutually agreed processes for monitoring the grant during the funding period. This generates confidence between partners. A funder or donor will want to be informed of any departure from the original plan; it may be necessary to re-negotiate this. Most funders will not want to withdraw funds during the funding period and will be committed to giving the project the best chances to succeed.

Although those in the restorative justice movement ideally want mainstream or long-term funding, the reality is that most charitable funders will tend to want to fund short-term pilot projects. Governments sometimes offer service agreements or contracts for limited periods. They should however be aware of the instability caused to an organisation and its staff if it constantly has to devote a large part of its efforts to seeking renewal of its funding.

These considerations all underpin the need for restorative justice managers to adopt a strategic approach to funding that embraces effective communications, the adoption of sound practice principles and the recruitment and retention of high calibre personnel as mediators, managers and board members.

c. Establishing co-operation

The importance of co-operation

Setting up a mediation service and ensuring that it runs smoothly, with an optimum level of suitable case referrals, requires close co-operation with existing criminal justice agencies. What has been said with regard to the creation of restorative justice services also holds true for their continuation. It is difficult to designate any one sure plan for successfully establishing co-operation; from experience in countries where restorative justice has taken hold we can only say – and repeat – that co-operation is of prime importance.

Prerequisites of co-operation

A prerequisite of good co-operation is a clear recognition of the function of the criminal justice system and its representatives, and also of the proper place of restorative justice in relation to the system. In other words, sound co-operation rests on a good understanding of one's own task and that of partner agencies.

Strategies to promote understanding

It is highly recommended to set up a routine of regular meetings of members of the referring agency and the practitioners of the mediation services. This is the case with most of the larger victim-offender mediation bureaus in Austria. In England, for example, the mediation service can be represented on the court users' committee, comprised of a group of judges, prosecutors, defending lawyers, probation and police officers, victim support workers, and others, which meet regularly in some courts for the discussion of local administrative problems.

Learning about mediation should also be part of the initial and in-service training of each of these professions. The ideas and preconceptions of professionals with regard to restorative justice are sometimes unrealistic. Either they perceive mediation as a predominantly rehabilitative process teaching the offender a lesson, or they regard it as a soft prelude to shaking hands and achieving an easy (maybe even lazy) agreement, without really addressing the offender's law-breaking and "wrongdoing". These misconceptions must be corrected in order to enjoy good co-operation. An introductory course, in which one can get a concrete "feeling" of the essence of mediation, should be offered and strongly recommended to professionals of the criminal justice system. The most effective way of making this come about is by doing mediation, in the form of some well-guided role-play that reveals clearly the differences between the two rationales – that of restorative justice and that of criminal justice.

A valuable device for achieving this is to set-up opportunities for state/public prosecutors and for judges to observe mediation sessions. In Austria, especially in Vienna, state prosecutors, including from abroad, have been invited to observe mediation sessions (provided the parties give their consent). Expert-interviews have shown that state prosecutors having the most thorough knowledge of the mediation procedure, its potential and its limitations make the most appropriate referrals.

Continuing co-operation

Seminars bringing together restorative justice practitioners and members of the criminal justice system, and which focus on specific themes relevant to those professions are another means of deepening mutual understanding and improving co-operation.

Ongoing co-operation must also be secured with members of related NGOs, especially with victim support agencies and other community agencies. Even if this appears difficult, the effort is worthwhile. We know from experience that otherwise misconceptions and hence bad feelings might arise that will severely impede the work of the restorative justice services.

The most important device remains the already mentioned routine meetings between members of the criminal justice system and practitioners from the restorative justice services, as well as members of other agencies.

In some countries, regular meetings between representatives of all agencies involved take place in the framework of permanent local steering committees. In Belgium, for example, a steering committee on restorative justice functions at the level of the judicial district. It can serve several mediation programmes at the subsequent stages of the criminal justice process. The common objectives and the roles and responsibilities of each partner organisation are written down in a protocol of co-operation.

Co-operation and autonomy

We want, once more, to stress the importance of the autonomy of restorative justice procedures in relation to the criminal justice system, and we strongly propose striving for what has been called the semi-internal position, namely a position of being connected to the criminal justice system while retaining the degree of autonomy that enables the spirit of restorativeness to unfold. With regard to the diversionary mode of restorative justice procedures, this relation can be called "conditional autonomy" (see section 2.a). What is the meaning of this concept?

Restorative justice services enjoy only conditional or temporary autonomy with regard to the criminal justice system. This ensures that the requirements and considerations with regard to due process are respected. Discretion concerning referral as well as the final discretion as to whether to continue or discontinue the legal process rests with the officers of the criminal justice system. The restorative justice procedure is inserted within these decisions. As soon as referral takes place, the restorative justice procedure is started, without interference from the state prosecutor (or the judge) and is detached from the course of criminal proceedings. Only when this truly alternative procedure is finished – and it should indeed constitute an alternative and not just a more informal, or secondary criminal procedure – the criminal justice system is invoked again and should come to the fore to exercise its discretionary powers.

In the case of serious crimes, the mediation procedure does not replace the court procedure but runs "alongside" it, as exemplified by the national Belgian Mediation for Redress Programme, co-ordinated by the NGOs Suggnomè (Flanders) and Médiante (Wallonia) (see section 1.d). The first function of the criminal procedure is to determine guilt or innocence, and then, if guilt is proved, to impose a sanction. It follows the rules of due process, the aim of which is to protect the perpetrator from wrongful conviction, undue state intervention and excessive sanctions. These sanctions have mixed aims: punishment, deterrence, rehabilitation, and so on. Restorative justice operates only where the involvement of the accused is not denied, and its first function is a different one: the repairing of harm. This is most important: the autonomy of the restorative justice services has to be preserved; and this implies that arrangements have to be constructed, argued for and tried out that guarantee maximum feasible autonomy – but also effective and efficient co-operation.

Chapter 4

Restorative justice and its participants

a. Volunteers and professionals

The involvement of members of the community in the mediation or conferencing process can make it more restorative. Both statutory agencies and NGOs can use volunteers as mediators, but NGOs are more likely to do so. Volunteers can be recruited from all sections of the community, reflecting the composition of the local population. Deliberate effort is needed, however, to recruit from as many minority groups as possible. They bring an understanding of local conditions, and also learn by participating, so that public understanding of crime and its background is increased. It has been found that with adequate training, support and supervision, they can mediate very competently, working to a high standard.

It has been suggested that victims and offenders are more appreciative of the contribution of people who are giving their time for the common good, although there is no definite evidence of this. Many volunteers have full-time jobs, and are available to mediate during evenings and weekends, which may also be more convenient for victims. Since they are unpaid, or paid less than professionals, it is more feasible to use two co-mediators, which can have advantages for the quality of mediation. They can support each other and evaluate each other's performance. Co-ordinators have to work hard to maintain a good level of commitment – to ensure, for example, that volunteers return telephone calls and take part in the necessary in-service training.

Some mediation services recruit mediators similarly from the local community, but pay them for each visit or mediation, sometimes a nominal honorarium, sometimes a full fee. This may extend the range of those who can become mediators. When incomes are low, people have to work overtime or take second jobs, and would not be able to give their time unless they were recompensed. For some, the extra income may be a stronger incentive than public spiritedness alone.

This group may be described as "paid lay mediators"; volunteers and paid lay mediators together can be called "community mediators".

Professional, full-time mediators can be expected to have undergone a more comprehensive training, measured in months rather than days, and probably with a more academic content including, for example, law, criminology, psychology and sociology. This has obvious advantages, but it may restrict the social range of people from which mediators are drawn; a firm policy is needed to ensure that mediations are conducted at times convenient to the participants, which may be outside normal office hours. Since they will be paid professional salaries, there will be a limit to the number that can be employed, and therefore to the number of cases they can handle. They may be employed by an NGO, or by a criminal justice agency such as the police or probation service; in that case, it is important that they adhere to the principles of restorative justice, and are not subordinated to those of the conventional system. In Austria, for example, mediators are part of the probation service but work only as mediators.

For both volunteer and professional mediators training is essential, as was shown in section 2.e, and a primary role of professionals will be to provide this. The co-ordination (management) of mediation services is also a task for professionals, whose training will need to include some administrative skills as well as an understanding of mediation.

Finally, in some places mediation is carried out by members of existing agencies: police, probation, court assistants *(Gerichtshelfer)* in Germany, youth offending teams (YOTs) in England and Wales, and so on. Here there are two dangers: one is that the values of the agency take precedence, as described above; the other is that the pressure of routine work simply does not allow officers to devote enough time to mediation training, to ensure that all suitable cases are referred to mediation by those responsible (such as prosecutors), nor to deal with those that are referred. The one possible advantage relates to cost: when officers are employed already, there is little extra cost if they do mediation rather than their other duties. Some extra funding should however be allocated to training, support and supervision by qualified mediators. If this is the only way of introducing restorative justice, mediations should be included in the assessment of the officers' performance, and this arrangement should be converted to a more whole-hearted restorative policy as soon as possible.

The best solution may be to combine the use of professionals and either volunteers or paid lay mediators. Straightforward cases could be handled by two community mediators; more complex ones by a professional and a community mediator working together, or by professionals only. In some cases, people who start as community mediators may change careers and be trained as professionals.

It is helpful to have a local organisation which is responsible for co-ordinating the work of mediators, including their recruitment, training, support and supervision. Local mediation services should ideally belong to an independent national association (or form one if it does not already exist), which would draw up standards in consultation with practitioners, co-ordinate training, maintain a system for accrediting mediation services, trainers and mediators, and provide support for local services.

b. Victim concerns

Since the rise of the victims' movement in the last thirty years, there has been growing awareness that the conventional criminal justice system has accorded no special status to victims of crime, as was shown in chapter 1. They are either disregarded after they have reported the offence, or treated as just another witness in the process of convicting or acquitting the accused. Advocates of restorative justice are keen to ensure that this process does not also re-victimise victims.

In a restorative system, the first concern should be with victims whose offenders are not known – the majority. Of these, many will have experienced inconvenience rather than trauma, but for those who have suffered serious harm, victim assistance should be available. For victims of violence, medical costs should be covered in countries which do not have a universal health service, and if possible additional compensation for pain and suffering, and extra costs not covered by the social welfare system. When the offender is known she or he can be required to contribute to compensation; but few offenders are able to make more than a symbolic payment.

Where the offender is known and admits involvement, a fully restorative process is possible. It is stressed once again that victims should be offered the opportunity to participate directly. Some mediation services have given priority to the rehabilitation of the offender – a tendency that is reinforced by political demands for reduced reconviction rates. This means that the service may appear to victims to be "using" them in the offender's interests rather than theirs. It is important to maintain close co-operation with victim support agencies (especially with vulnerable victims, for example in domestic violence cases). One way of doing this is to invite a representative of a victim support organisation to join the management committee of the mediation service.

There are several possible problems from the victim's point of view. It has been suggested that victims may find that taking a decision on whether to participate is stressful; they "may feel guilty if they choose not to participate yet anxious if they do".[1] There is however no evidence that such feelings are widespread. Pressure to take part could be subtle: "If you decline, you are the bad guy" (Umbreit, Coates and Vos, 2001). Victims may feel that they are insufficiently prepared for the mediation session, or are given unrealistic expectations about the extent to which they can participate in the process. Some are not contacted at all. This is due to poor practice, or in some cases legislation which does not permit victims to have adequate participation in the decision-making process. There have been reports of victims not being contacted at all, sometimes because social workers are not accustomed to dealing with victims, sometimes because of concern over data protection. Victims' privacy should be respected, but this should not deny them the opportunity to take part in a process which many find beneficial.

In a mediation session (and especially a conference), could the victim be outnumbered and feel overawed by the offender and his or her relatives? This is a possibility, though here again there are no reports that it is widespread. Facilitators can guard against it by the choice and preparation of participants for the conference, and by setting ground rules and ensuring that they are followed. Once again

---

1. Reeves and Mulley (2000), quoted by Strang (2002: 206).

New Zealand[1] suggests a safeguard: a victim "may be accompanied by any reasonable number of persons (being members of his or her family ... or any other persons) who attend the conference for the purpose of providing support to that victim".

Finally, should victims be supported by lawyers? As has already been noted, anyone involved in a legal process has the right to "legal assistance of his own choosing" (European Convention on Human Rights, Article 6.3(c)) free if they cannot afford it. Legal representation would however be contrary to the concept of restorative justice, in which all participants speak for themselves, and should aim for a win-win solution, not a win-lose result that is traditional among lawyers. For this reason it is generally assumed that lawyers should not take part in mediation sessions. It has been suggested that lawyers with a good understanding of restorative justice (which would require specialist training) should be available before and/or after mediation sessions.

c. Offender concerns

Concerns about safeguards for offenders cannot in fact be completely separated from victim concerns. Since restorative justice practices deal with relations between people, we are always confronted with two halves of a process. This two-way orientation constitutes one of the most important differences between restorative justice procedures and the conventional criminal procedure that clearly focuses on the offender.

On the other hand, this criminal process frequently ends by imposing punishment on the offender, and has therefore established safeguards to protect him or her from unjust conviction or punishment, and to guarantee his or her personal rights and freedoms. Victim-offender mediation and conferencing are informal processes based on consent, leading not to punishment but to reparation; consequently they have few such safeguards installed. Only insofar as mediation, as a diversionary measure, is linked to the criminal justice system, do these safeguards remain there – in the background – to be invoked whenever the process of mediation is halted by one of the parties.

This is different where the restorative justice service is not bound to the criminal justice system at all but is carried out as independent community mediation, handling all kinds of conflicts that are brought to this service. Here the needs and vulnerabilities of both parties have to be attended to from the very beginning.

Inside the victim-offender mediation or conferencing procedure the principle of proportionality can be invoked to protect the offender from undue (disproportionate) burdens or obligations that he or she might be asked to undertake to compensate the victim and make amends. It is suggested that this principle should be applied in one direction only, that is, to reduce reparation that appears excessive, but not to increase it if both parties appear to be content with it. It is the task of the

---

1. Children, Young Persons and Their Families Amendment (1994), section 37(2), quoted by Roche (2003: 91 footnote).

mediator to attend to this principle by extending to both parties the working principles of respect, recognition and impartiality, which guide the mediation procedure (as stated in section 1.e).

This appears in general to have worked very well, but the good intentions of mediators are not a guarantee of good practice in every case. An offender, especially a young and inarticulate one, who feels that he or she was not treated with respect, or was intimidated in the process, or has agreed to a disproportionate amount of reparation, may not dare to make a complaint afterwards. A mediator may have failed to follow the highest standards. There needs to be a system to prevent such unfairness as far as possible, and to put the situation right if it occurs.

The first step towards preventing situations of this kind is to train mediators. They should be made aware of these issues and shown how to avoid them. Co-mediation, where it is used, provides an opportunity for mediators to guide each other and asses each session afterwards. Courts can ask questions to ensure that the process was as restorative as possible. Participants, both offenders and victims, should be prepared for the process and informed about what to expect and what they can do if they feel that their expectations were not met.

The same concerns mentioned in relation to the support by lawyers to victims (see section 4.b) can be expressed in relation to the support by lawyers to offenders. In New Zealand, youth advocates are attached to courts and funded by them; they advise young people but do not represent them, and in the more serious cases the agreed plan has to be approved by the judge (Akester, 2000). It has been suggested that the presence of supporters is itself a safeguard. In New South Wales, Australia, there is also a free legal advice helpline for children (Roche, 2003: 88-93).

Offenders who fail to complete their agreed reparation should also be dealt with restoratively. They should be given the chance to explain why they have not done so (for example, their circumstances may have changed, or an agency may not have provided the support or treatment that they need), and to recommit themselves to the original agreement or a re-negotiated one. Only if they still fail to comply should they be returned to court.

The mediation procedure is neither victim-centred nor offender-centred but centred on what has happened and is happening between the parties. But it is the infringement of the victim's rights that sets in motion the intervention of criminal law agencies in the first place. Therefore focusing on the offender is usually built into the "system" and the policy of referring agencies. It is also to a large degree built into the perceptions of the restorative justice services. It might therefore become one of the most important tasks of a restorative justice service to emphasise – especially in the beginning – the "change of lenses" (Zehr, 1995) to bring the victim more into focus.

With regard to the lack of legal safeguards in the mediation procedure, some authors have called for a specific appeal procedure to be installed. It would allow those who think that they have received unfair treatment to voice their complaint and to be invited to resolve it informally, or by independent mediation. If that was

d. Public opinion and the role of the media

In addition to motivating and mobilising co-operating agencies (see section 3.a), gaining and holding the support of the public is of prime importance when setting-up restorative justice services.

Public attitude and opinions

Considerable fear has been expressed that the offer of mediation will meet with the public's distrust and even resistance. These apprehensions arise from the perception that the public is punitive, which is an over-simplification. They are based partly on reports in popular newspapers, for which an apparently lenient sentence makes an easy headline. This is however reinforced by the assumptions on which some scientific research is based. People responding to questionnaires and presented with questions such as "How much punishment is appropriate?" or "Should a given offender receive punishment or rehabilitation?", tend to choose answers likely to be on a punitive-lenient spectrum. A recent book on attitudes to punishment, for example, makes only a passing reference to restorative justice (Roberts and Hough, 2002). An international crime survey reported on fifty-eight countries but asked only about "fine, prison, community service, suspended sentence or another sentence" as the options for a young recidivist burglar (Mayhew and van Kesteren, 2002). All of these are punitive options, although (as the authors point out) community service may be regarded in different ways – as reparative, rehabilitative or as "hard labour". In most of Europe, community service was preferred to prison (with the notable exception of two Anglophone countries, the United Kingdom and Malta).

But different questions produce different responses. Some surveys have asked only about reparation; others have included the element of victim-offender dialogue that is the distinguishing feature of restorative justice. Some have distinguished victims from non-victims, and found that victims do not tend to be more punitive: they want some form of redress. In 1982 a survey of burglary victims found that they generally wanted the offender to repay his or her "debt" in a useful way, through restitution or working for the community, and remarks like "Prison does no good to anyone" were common. In the same year a survey of nearly 1 000 respondents found that 85% thought it was a good idea to make some offenders do community service instead of going to prison, and 66% wanted to make them pay compensation to their victims. In 1984, before victim-offender mediation was well known, the British Crime Survey (BCS) asked victims whether they would have accepted meeting the offender in order "to agree a way in which the offender could make repayment for what he had done", and 49% said they would; another 20% would have liked an agreement without a meeting – 69% in all. In the 1998 BCS a different question was asked: 41% would have accepted the chance "to meet their offender in the presence of a third party ... to ask offenders why they had committed the offence and tell them how it had made them feel" (Wright, 1989; Maguire and Corbett, 1987; Mattinson and Mirrlees-Black, 2000).

In Germany, surveys of the general population found that most people would like minor crimes to be dealt with by reparation; many would like this arranged independently rather than through the criminal justice process. Victims were not more punitive than non-victims. There was more acceptance of victim/offender mediation as a diversion from the criminal trial, rather than as one of a range of sentencing options. If reparation were made, the level of punishment proposed was lower. One survey found that the general public was less punitive than criminal justice professionals, except for the most serious crimes (Dölling and Henninger, 1998, 360ff). In the Hamburg victim survey, Sessar (1992) found quite remarkable results with regard to the respondents' wide preference for *Wiedergutmachung* (reparation) over *Strafe* (punishment). Interestingly, the representatives of the criminal justice system, especially state prosecutors, showed the most pronounced punitive attitudes. Later research has found similar attitudes (Kilchling and Kaiser, 1996) (see also section 1.g).

Apart from surveys, practical experience in mediation projects has shown a surprisingly high readiness of victims to participate and declare that they renounce any further prosecution after a mediation procedure in which they have come to an agreement and obtained reparation. For many of these participants, mediation appears the ordinary and "normal" way to deal with the aftermath of crime. Interestingly, both research evidence and "anecdotal" evidence reveals a tendency that runs counter to the common expectation: they show that people's "restorative" attitudes (as far as petty and middle-range offences are concerned) strongly increase when they are closer to the experience of victimisation and are confronted with a concrete offer of receiving reparation, an explanation and a serious apology from the perpetrator. It has also been found (see section 1.g) that the satisfaction rate among those who have taken part in victim-offender mediation and conferencing is in almost all cases very high, provided that the process is conducted well. It may therefore be expected that its popularity will increase as more people take part, and it becomes more widely known.

Legislators and administrators may thus be confident that restorative justice can be presented to the public as a measure that is neither tough nor lenient but appropriate and reasonable, an expression of common sense.

The role of the media

Mediation services are strongly recommended to develop and implement a communications strategy. More specifically, we would advise administrators and policy makers to establish a relationship of trust with a few journalists (from both print and electronic media) who can be regularly provided with concrete accounts of the mediation service and its work, and – most important – with case histories (subject to either anonymity or to the consent of both parties). It is not enough to issue just one press release and have done with it. Also in this respect an ongoing process is required to provide a continuing stream of information.

As with many other pieces of information, schools provide an important channel not only for disseminating information but also for exerting some influence on public attitudes. Again it needs careful preparation as well as perseverance to make an impression that lasts.

Arguments that have proved powerful

The best argument for using restorative justice is not an argument but a successful case history, preferably one where the offence was relatively serious, and where the victim, the offender or both experienced a change of attitude as a result of the process.

After that, the strongest argument is the effect on victims. Advocates of restorative justice emphasise that it begins by trying to repair the harm done to them. As has been mentioned already, many victims welcome the opportunity to see the offender, to express their anger and ask questions. Unlike courts, mediation centres offer a less formal atmosphere that is centred on victims' needs. This enables victims to ask questions; often the offender is the only person who can answer them.

Although many victims put these concerns above reparation, the mediation process usually enables those who *do* want reparation to obtain it more quickly, and offenders who have agreed to compensation have been found to be more likely to pay it – and more quickly. In view of the neglect of victims' point of view and needs, orientation towards the victim cannot be stressed enough.

After a mediation process, as compared with a court hearing, more victims overcome the effects of crime and several studies have found that fewer of them fear being targeted by the offender again.

Some arguments relate to the offender, for example, "Would you agree that it makes sense to ask the offender to make up for what he or she has done?" Reflective people also accept that the harmful effects of prisons outweigh the rehabilitative programmes that are available to a minority of prisoners, except for those who are a serious threat to the public. Another popular idea is that "offenders should be answerable (or accountable) for the harm they caused". This should not, however, be presented as a form of retributive punishment. Facing the victim personally can make the effects of the act more visible and can support the offender in taking responsibility towards the future.

Mediation is generally organised more quickly than a court hearing. When it takes place before the hearing, it saves the court's time so that the backlog of serious cases can be reduced, and therefore saves money.

Another aspect, which has not yet been given enough attention, is crime reduction. The non-confrontational atmosphere also encourages offenders to talk about the pressures that led them towards crime. When the community has been made aware of these, it can take action as part of its crime-reduction strategy.

CHAPTER 5

EVALUATION AND FURTHER DEVELOPMENT

a. Issues in programme evaluation and research

In this section we shall consider the meaning of research, and different types of mainly empirical research (research on effects, research on processes and research that accompanies implementation). After a review of the experience of different European countries, some problems involved in designing evaluative research are discussed. A section on theoretical research proposes three groups of questions, and a theoretical research agenda.

The meaning of research

Committee of Ministers Recommendation No. R (99) 19 on mediation in penal matters, which was presented in chapter 2, ends with the principle that: "Member States should promote research on, and evaluation of, mediation in penal matters". Research is concerned, inter alia, with procedures of objective description and assessment, as the explanatory memorandum explains: "Research is essential for gaining knowledge on the functioning of mediation. ... There is a need for evaluative research on mediation in penal matters, in particular as it is still in its initial stages in most European countries".

Although in this section we are mainly looking at *empirical* research on restorative justice practices, *theoretical* or fundamental research is of vital importance as well. Both types of research are intertwined. A theoretical contextualisation – for example in respect of the relationship of restorative justice with retributive justice – can help us to understand how mediation practice and policy are developing as they are, and in which direction they can be oriented.

As regards the different types of empirical research, our interest in a particular type of research, for example on the outcome of mediation, reflects an underlying vision on the essentials of restorative justice, and justice in general. Three main streams in restorative justice research can be discerned in this regard. The first puts the emphasis on the instrumental function of the new method (mediation as a means to achieve some observable effects); the second underlines that mediation is essentially a process, more precisely its participatory nature and its potential for community involvement as a value and an end in itself; and the third combines research with practice, by studying a project as it is implemented.

An example of the first kind of research is evaluation that is designed to inform on victim-offender satisfaction in a differentiated way; this will need a careful research design, which in turn needs the co-operation of a well-established and well-equipped research institution. The same holds for the second type, which is up to now only sparingly applied in this field, namely qualitative process analysis that studies communication between the mediator and the parties, and communication between the parties themselves. This type of research will help us to learn more about the concrete implementation of restorative processes and the way they affect men and women participating in these processes.

We want to emphasise the advantages to be derived from the third type, accompanying research, when it begins at the time a restorative justice (pilot) project is set up. It requires, first, a well-designed method of collecting data that is both comprehensive and easy to handle by the practitioners. Second, there should be from the beginning provisions and arrangements for ongoing contacts between different groups participating in the project and the research team. Third, the researcher should convey to the other actors that research will not be "on them" or about them but "with them". Their voice and their (self-) interpretations of the progress of the programme are to become an integral part of the research effort. Provisions should also be made early on for the researcher to design and to establish a monitoring and follow-up procedure that will maintain some sort of continued evaluation after the pilot project phase is finished.

Accompanying research is closely linked to what is sometimes called action research. In action research, researchers join practitioners in elaborating the initial concept of the project.

The advantages of comprehensive accompanying research consist in presenting an evaluation both of the process and of the (short-term) outcomes of mediation, meaning the content and the type of agreement reached – as well as of the fulfilment of restitution agreements. In addition, it is intended to exert an immediate influence on the process of setting-up a new service. It provides a useful tool both for project development and for underpinning the request for establishing, broadening and financing restorative justice services by way of producing sets of scientifically grounded arguments.

Looking at the experience of different countries

There are considerable differences between European countries as to the amount of research on victim-offender mediation and conferencing that has been undertaken (Aertsen, Vanfraechem and Willemsens, 2004). There are, on the one hand, countries where almost no empirical research is done, even when many cases are dealt with by mediation every year. There are, on the other hand, countries with a rich tradition of empirical research. In these countries, the types of empirical research evolve at the same time the practice is developing and restorative mediation is implemented on a larger scale. In the early stage of development, descriptive and action research dominate. Evaluative research is of utmost importance from the very beginning as well, but an in-depth and comparative evaluation is usually only possible after several years of operation. We have already pointed out the importance of programme evaluation in the course of setting-up restorative justice services (section 3.a).

Research and evaluation are not exclusively done from outside the existing mediation programmes, in the form of research projects on specific topics carried out by specialised institutions such as universities or government research departments. Many mediation and conferencing services issue annual reports and other analytical documents, which offer a multitude of relevant data. Within – and even between – countries, annual figures from mediation services on the number and nature of cases, characteristics of victims and offenders, the way of handling the case by judicial authorities and others, should be collected in a way that will ensure comparability (using common definitions, categories, etc.) Ongoing monitoring research, for example, has been done in Germany since 1993, where a consortium of universities on behalf of the federal minister of justice is gathering and analysing data on mediation practice on an annual basis (Kerner, Hartmann and Lenz, 2003).

Worth mentioning here is the Cost Action A21 project on "Restorative justice developments in Europe".[1] Cost Action A21 concerns a network of researchers who study research results and methods related to victim-offender mediation and conferencing in European countries. The general aim of the Cost Action A21 project, which runs for a period of four years (2002-06), is to "enhance and to deepen knowledge on theoretical and practical aspects of restorative justice in Europe, with a view on supporting implementation strategies in a scientifically sound way". The work of this project is organised through the exchange and discussion in three thematic working groups, namely on evaluative research, policy oriented research and theoretical research. We shall refer to its programme in more detail below.

In looking at the experience of different countries, we find that some kind of programme evaluation has been going on (or is still going on) almost everywhere. Most frequently it has been research in connection with pilot projects. Extensive accompanying research was done in the course of the two Austrian pilot projects, which were forerunners in establishing victim-offender mediation as a diversionary measure based on legislation and thereby establishing a nationwide practice. A similar type of accompanying research was associated with the Belgium Mediation for Redress Project (1993-95) and was carried out by the research group "Penology and victimology" of the Catholic University of Leuven (financed partly by the King Baudoin Foundation and partly by the Belgium Ministry of Justice). It was applied at the earlier stages of experimenting with victim-offender mediation in Finland.[2]

---

[1]. Cost is a European intergovernmental partnership of thirty-four countries and stands for Co-operation in the field of Scientific and Technical Research. In 2002, a project (an action) on restorative justice research was approved. For more information on Cost and on Cost Action A21 see: http://cost.cordis.lu.
[2]. Action research accompanying the first mediation project of the city of Vantaa; this research was carried out by Juhani Iivari and financed by the Academy of Finland.

Research of this kind has also been carried out in Poland. Between 1997 and 1999 the Institute of Law Studies of the Polish Academy of Sciences carried out programme evaluation research accompanying the pilot project of victim-offender mediation for young offenders. It was based on documentation (following a questionnaire developed by the researchers) as well as an analysis of court files and a questionnaire sent out to the "mediation parties". A similar approach was followed with regard to the second pilot project, which involved adult offenders and their victims – this time organised by the Institute for the Administration of Justice, affiliated to the Ministry of Justice.

Interestingly, Norway, the country supporting nationwide coverage of victim-offender mediation with a remarkable high caseload, introduced its model of victim-offender mediation centres organised by the municipalities after some experimentation but without undertaking systematic scientific evaluation. Not until five years after introducing the Act on Mediation (1991) was an evaluation commissioned by the Norwegian Ministry of Justice and carried out by the Institute of Criminology at the University of Oslo.

In Catalonia, accompanying research on a pilot project was commissioned by the Catalan Department of Justice and carried out by practitioners and researchers of the mediation team. An assessment of a series of pilot projects was also done by the Council of Crime Prevention in Sweden. The United Kingdom – as with restorative justice practices and programmes in general – presents a highly diversified picture. The type of research carried out has changed over the years depending on the changing policy context within which restorative justice initiatives operate, "which has had important implications both for the kind of empirical research that has been undertaken, and also its desirability in the eyes of potential funders" (Dignan, 2004, 1). Most stand-alone projects that have been launched since the mid-1980s have been evaluated, sometimes by way of action research (as was the case with one of the first projects that used mediation and reparation in conjunction with diversion from prosecution of adults as well as young offenders) and often applying a quite complex research design.

Problems of designing evaluation research

These examples raise several questions which confront programme administrators and policy makers.

A scientifically valid and reliable evaluation cannot do without a proper control group. Strictly speaking this control group must start from the same conditions as the experimental (project) group. To achieve this it needs random assignment of cases to the experimental group and to the control group. Random assignment would in practice mean that the referring agency (the police, the state prosecutor) would place every other case (of a certain type, for example where an individual victim is involved) with the control group, while numbers 1, 3, 5, and so on would go to the restorative justice programme – regardless of the specific nature of the case. Any other method of constructing a control group (for example the one applied in the Austrian study) would produce a pre-selection effect, as it would be the agency's assessment of the circumstances of the case that would determine its placement.

Although, from a scientific point of view random assignment guarantees the most "pure", reliable and valid results and thus the strongest arguments, this will only very rarely become possible to realise. The method of random assignment will encounter severe limitations and might not be compatible at all with the rationale of the criminal justice system and even more so where there exists only a small margin of discretion for the agencies of the criminal justice system, in particular, the police and the state prosecutors, who are bound by the principle of legality. Thus there will always be a pre-selection bias, insofar as the assignment of a case to a certain kind of innovative handling always implies the selection of those cases that are regarded as appropriate by the responsible person/actor.

We drew attention earlier to a meta-analysis on "The effectiveness of restorative justice practices" commissioned by the Research and Statistics Division of the Department of Justice of Canada (Latimer, Dowden and Muise, 2001). The existence of a control group (though not necessarily randomly assigned) was a prerequisite. The achievement of the analysis consists in strictly comparing the effects of restorative justice programmes with the effects shown in the respective control groups. This analysis showed that compared to traditional non-restorative approaches, restorative justice was found to be more successful at achieving what were defined as its major goals (summarised in section 1.g).

But it also pointed out that the positive results of the meta-analysis are tempered by the self-selection bias that comes into the picture because of the voluntary nature of restorative justice programmes, even when the referring agency has applied random assignment to "treatment" or "comparison" groups. It may be said that the victims interviewed had chosen to take part in mediation and were therefore predisposed in favour of it, but the high satisfaction rates do at least show that their expectations were generally fulfilled, and when they were not, it was often because of poor practice rather than the failings of restorative justice itself (Strang, 2002). It can also be argued that the introduction of restorative justice is justified even if it only benefits those who have chosen it, provided that this is not outweighed by disadvantages for others.

Restorative justice research, though extensive, has been criticised because very few studies have used random allocation, and some do not even have a comparison group. We regard it as important to point out these inherent problems of designing restorative justice research and of interpreting results. But we also think that it suffices to be aware of them and take them into account.

Latimer and his colleagues also mentioned the critique voiced against predominant reliance on recidivism studies. The reduction of recidivism rates of restorative justice programmes compared to conventional programmes was not overwhelming. And it was argued that this is not surprising given the fact that restorative justice interventions are mostly time-limited events. In addition it seems important to emphasise that restorative justice processes aim at "restoration", the setting-right of the harm and suffering inflicted on the victim, and on the breach and disturbance of social bonds and relationships. Research should therefore to a large degree be designed to look into the processes of restoration and healing, and to identify the factors influencing these processes and their effects on both victim and offender.

Theoretical research

The term "restorative justice" was coined after the development of its practice. It draws upon a wide range of academic disciplines, which include theology, ethics and moral philosophy. Related to these are political and legal theory, and aesthetics and rhetoric. On the empirical side, psychology, sociology, anthropology and history each have a part to play. In studies today, much writing crosses the boundaries of disciplines and sub-disciplines. It is therefore sometimes difficult to categorise theoretical works decisively.

So what does it mean to have different theories of restorative justice? The different types of theory serve different purposes. Some are concerned with telling us what restorative justice is: throwing light on what practitioners do, including empirical evaluation and the role restorative justice plays in the criminal-penal justice archipelago, and so forth. Others are mostly concerned with defining what restorative justice *should* do, what part it *should* play.

A number of major issues arise from the development of restorative justice. Broadly speaking we may identify them as a range of grouped questions, as follows.

First, what is restorative justice? What does it mean? What practices are restorative and which are not? Is it a set of practices, a grand theory of justice, a theory – partial or otherwise – of law itself? These are questions of definition and reference.

Second, what justifies restorative justice as a practice or as a theory? In what normative or spiritual frame or frames of reference does or can restorative justice exist? Is restorative justice to be justified on a universal basis or within the traditions of particular communities? These are ethical, legal, political and theological explorations.

Third, what is happening in restorative justice? How do we make sense of practice? Are practitioners doing what they say they are doing? Is it of any use or value? How shall we evaluate restorative justice? These are empirical, qualitative and quantitative questions.

These key issues that restorative justice theory has to address have been identified by the Cost Action A21 working group on theoretical research. The following is a résumé of some of these issues.

What are the aims of restorative justice, and what is its justification ethically, politically, legally and spiritually? What is the relationship between restorative justice and the legal system? What are the limits of restorative justice vis-à-vis the criminal justice system? How does the practice of mediation affect principles relating to the protection of the accused, such as due process and confidentiality? How should restorative justice affect the traditional sanctioning function of the criminal justice system? And how will it affect principles such as proportionality and equality of treatment in sentencing?

We have to deal with the implications of bringing back the victim and the private element of the wrongdoing into the criminal arena. What does this mean for the division of private and public law? This has implications for the way in which the event is perceived by the court – as crime or conflict – and also how the parties are regarded. To whom does the event belong?

We also have to deal with the question of whether different principles or considerations apply in mediation in which children are parties, most usually as offenders, but also as victims.

The emergence of restorative justice at a time of increased political activism in the field of antisocial behaviour, repression of crime and increased social surveillance and control requires critical theoretical treatment. We have to consider the implications of drawing the community's interests into the practice of restorative justice, and the need to uphold civil liberties.

Finally, we have to consider the psychological, legal, moral and spiritual dimensions of a number of significant themes that the practice of restorative justice brings into new and controversial focus: the nature of guilt, responsibility, shame and remorse, and the place of forgiveness.

b. Working toward comparability

The question of comparability is closely linked to the setting-up of research that evaluates a newly designed restorative justice programme. It is a requirement of European and global developments in this field. Working toward comparability will contribute to the individual programme's standing as well as to the further development of restorative justice in a wider cross-national context.

In this section, the specific contribution of national programmes to this effort will be outlined on the basis of the agenda derived from the goals set out by the scientific programme for the Cost Action 21 "Restorative justice developments in Europe". As this is work in progress and the Cost Action 21 project is still in its first stages, these contributions will mainly provide the ground for future comparability.

They will include:
– a comprehensive description of the basic features of the national criminal justice system (several Grotius projects have made a contribution in that direction by asking each country to provide descriptions of (parts of) their justice systems);
– an overview of the statistical information concerning the functioning of the criminal justice system in general (see also the *European Sourcebook of Crime and Criminal Justice Statistics*, Killias et al., 2003);

- a description of the way restorative justice has been or is intended to be fitted into this system;
- a detailed description of the programme and the way it is to work;
- information about the documentation system used by the restorative justice service;
- information about the data collection system used by the restorative justice programme;
- information on the type of evaluation research applied;
- information on the methods of evaluation research that will be used.

Since an effort will be made in the course of the Cost project to harmonise national recording systems, it will be up to the Cost participants to set up common criteria that will help to collect comparable data and information.

As concerns evaluation research and instruments it is highly recommended to have an overview of the most important research done to date, concentrating perhaps on meta-analyses and the methods applied. Research should not fall behind already established standards.

What has already been said with regard to the setting up of restorative justice services also applies to the realm of research: international exchange with colleagues from other countries is indispensable. Seminars dedicated to specific topics will provide an opportunity to discuss research methods and also issues of comparability.

One prerequisite is to ensure that definitions are comparable, including such basic questions as "What is a 'case'?" A second is to agree on the translation of terminology, for which Julex, a dictionary of legal terms (see p. 60) should be enlarged and updated. Thirdly, compatible computer programmes would simplify the task. Finally, routine follow-up of cases is desirable not only for purposes of monitoring but in the interest of the participants themselves; but this takes time and therefore money, and needs to be included in budgets.

To summarise: comparability can only emerge from a thorough knowledge of the specificities of each country. And to arrive at a real understanding of them we need to examine their context. Only when we are able to fully perceive and understand the complexity and diversity of different national situations can we begin to do comparative studies. National programmes can help with this and a joint effort by all of those working in this field will be required.

c. International co-operation

Throughout, this guide has emphasised the importance of international exchange, in particular, comparability between restorative justice developments in different countries. This exchange and international co-operation in general should not only support research objectives, but good practice and policy development as well. Many problems, certainly at the initial stage of development of restorative justice, are common to several countries. Neighbouring countries provide new ideas and creative solutions for problems. Restorative justice initiatives often start at local level, before they inspire other initiators in the same country and abroad.

The following examples demonstrate the effectiveness of international co-operation in restorative justice matters, and are mainly oriented towards practice and policy developments. They also show further perspectives in international co-operation.

From informal meetings to supranational policy

First, there are many forms of bilateral or regional co-operation between countries. There have been exchanges of practical experience and co-operation in research between Austria and Germany. Germany provided support for the development of mediation and the training of mediators in Poland. Norway and Denmark offered help to Albania, Austria to Slovenia, and the United Kingdom to Czech Republic and Russia Federation. The Nordic countries, Norway, Sweden, Finland and Denmark, engage in regional consultations as part of the Nordic Forum for Mediation.[1] Plans have been made for similar regional consultations between a number of east European countries.

Existing European or international organisations have focused on victim-offender mediation. This is the case of the Conférence permanente européenne de la Probation (CEP),[2] the European umbrella organisation for probation services. Its annual conference in 1997 in Wittenberg (Germany) was completely dedicated to this topic, and later on, seminars on restorative justice approaches were organised. The European Forum for Victim Services[3] dedicated some of its annual gatherings to restorative justice as well. Penal Reform International, an international NGO, is a prominent partner in developing restorative justice practices in eastern European countries and beyond.[4]

Particularly important in the area of victim-offender mediation has been a number of activities of the Council of Europe. In addition to organising conferences and giving support to existing structures to initiate mediation services in parts of eastern Europe through the setting-up of training programmes, the Council issued Committee of Ministers Recommendation No. R (99) 19 concerning mediation in penal matters. This guide frequently refers to its principles.

Also in 1999, the European Commission called for additional research and pilot projects in victim-offender mediation, in the "Communication on crime victims in the European Union: Reflections on standards and action".[5] This communication marked a contribution to the further implementation of the Action Plan on the establishment of an Area of Freedom, Security and Justice, adopted on 3 December 1998.[6]

---

1. See www.n-f-m.org.
2. See www.cep-probation.org.
3. See www.euvictimservices.org.
4. See www.penalreform.org.
5. COM (1999) 349 final, Brussels, 14 July 1999.
6. Action Plan of the Council and the Commission on how best to implement the provisions of the Treaty of Amsterdam on an Area of Freedom, Security and Justice, OJ C19/1, 23.1.99.

Later, the Council of the European Union took a similar step by adopting the above-mentioned "Council framework decision on the standing of victims in criminal proceedings" on 15 March 2001.[1] The framework decision, an initiative of Portugal, obliges member states of the European Union to adapt their national laws so as to afford victims of crime a minimum level of protection. The document also contains a specific provision on mediation in criminal cases, as described in section 2.b of this guide. Notwithstanding the vague wording of article 10 on mediation, its importance should not be underestimated. For the first time a binding European Union legal text recognises victim-offender mediation as a practice that can benefit victims and which should be in operation within the next few years.

During the last few years, the European Commission has also funded several Grotius projects to partnerships of organisations from different countries, which focused on specific themes within restorative justice and victim-offender mediation.

A Council of the European Union decision was proposed by the Belgian government in 2002 to set up a "European network of national contact points for restorative justice".[2] This official European structure, when adopted, should facilitate the implementation and further development of restorative justice mainly at a policy and judicial level.

A final international instrument, useful for developing restorative justice at the national level, is the "United Nations basic principles on the use of restorative justice programmes in criminal matters" (see also section 2.a).[3] These principles were initially prepared by an alliance of NGOs. Sponsored by the Canadian government and co-sponsored by forty other countries, the principles were approved as a draft resolution by the UN Crime Commission in April 2000. In July 2000, the Economic and Social Council issued UN Resolution 2000/14 to step up adoption of the resolution. In December 2000, the UN Secretary-General invited governments, intergovernmental organisations and NGOs to give their views on the desirability and utility of developing this resolution further. On the basis these viewpoints, a committee of experts (Canada, October 2001) drafted a document which formed the basis for the endorsement of the basic principles by the Economic and Social Council in July 2002 (Van Ness, 2003).

Two initiatives should be mentioned with regard to international research networks. The first is the "International network for research on restorative justice for juveniles", which primarily organises annual conferences on restorative justice research. During a first conference in 1997, the Declaration of Leuven on the Advisability of Promoting the Restorative Approach to Juvenile Crime was

---

1. Council Framework Decision of 15 March 2001 on the standing of victims in criminal proceedings, OJ L82, 22.3.2001, pp. 1-4.
2. Initiative of the Kingdom of Belgium with a view to the adoption of a Council Decision setting up a European network of national contact points for restorative justice, OJ C 242/20, 8.10.2002.
3. UN Commission on Crime Prevention and Criminal Justice, *Restorative justice. Report of the Secretary-General*, Vienna, E/CN.15.2002/5/Add.1.

adopted.[1] The second initiative is that of Cost Action 21 on "Restorative justice developments in Europe" (see p. 81).[2]

Another valuable initiative is the European master in mediation international training programme. This is a postgraduate educational programme, started in 1999, that focuses on international exchange and applies to different fields of practice, such as family mediation, school mediation, community mediation, victim-offender mediation, environmental mediation, international mediation, mediation in commercial disputes, and so on. It offers advanced programmes for students who have already acquired a certain level of practical experience in one of the above-mentioned fields. The programme is organised through a partnership of several European universities and is co-ordinated by the University Institute Kurt Bösch in Sion, Switzerland.[3]

A European forum

After a preparatory period of two years, facilitated by a European Union Grotius grant, the European Forum for Victim-Offender Mediation and Restorative Justice was launched at the end of 2000.[4] The European forum is an NGO, established according to Belgian law. Its general aim is to help set up and develop victim-offender mediation and other restorative justice practices throughout Europe. To achieve this, it seeks to:

– promote the international exchange of information and mutual assistance;

– promote the development of effective restorative justice policies, services and legislation;

– explore and develop the theoretical basis of restorative justice;

– stimulate research; and

– assist the development of principles, ethics, training and good practice.

In addition, Article 6 of the forum's constitution defines the following actions:

– to promote dialogue between practitioners, policymakers and researchers;

– to support public education aimed at increasing awareness about issues for victims, offenders and the community;

– to make representation to and/or liaise with European and international institutions or organisations, including the Council of Europe, the European Union and relevant NGOs;

---

1. International Network for Research on Restorative Justice for Juveniles (1997, Declaration of Leuven on the Advisability of Promoting the Restorative Approach to Juvenile Crime; made on the occasion of the first International Conference on "Restorative Justice for Juveniles. Potentialities, Risks and Problems for Research", Leuven, May 12-14, 1997, *European Journal on Criminal Policy and Research*, 5.4, 118-122.
2. See http://cost.cordis.lu.
3. See http://www.iukb.ch.
4. See http://www.euforumrj.org.

– to raise, hold and administer funds and disburse such funds to further its work.

Although the main focus of the European forum is on mediation in criminal matters and related restorative developments, such as family group conferencing, links have been made to other fields of mediation. The forum is concerned with both juveniles and adults and its target group consists of mediators and mediation services; policy makers; and researchers and criminal justice practitioners all over Europe.

Contacts with other regions are being further developed. One of the sister organisations in this regard is the North American Victim Offender Mediation Association (Voma).[1] The forum also considers other European and international organisations working in the field of victim assistance, offender care and restorative justice as important partners in realising its objectives. One of the tasks of the European forum is to influence policy-making in the field of restorative justice at national and supranational levels.

Its organisational structure consists of a general meeting, a board and committees. Through committees, the forum tries to actively engage as many members as possible. The objective of the Research Committee is to propose, promote and support research projects in areas related to restorative justice practices and theory. The Practice and Training Committee exchanges information on mediation methodology and training programmes. The Information Committee collects and disseminates information on practices, policy and legislation in the field of restorative justice in European countries. This information is published and updated by the committee. The Communications Committee is responsible for the internal and external communication with(in) the forum and for organising the bi-annual conferences. These four committees work closely together with the board and the secretariat, which is located at the University of Leuven (Belgium) The European forum publishes a newsletter tri-annually, for which an editorial board is responsible.

The work of the European forum is funded by the national governments of several European countries, through membership fees and particular projects. In 2003, two forum projects were granted funding through the European Commission Agis programme. The first of these projects deals with training for judges and public prosecutors and for mediators, and the second supports the implementation of restorative justice in central and eastern Europe.

---

1. See http://www.euforumrj.org.

Appendix

RECOMMENDATION No. R (99) 19
OF THE COMMITTEE OF MINISTERS TO MEMBER STATES
CONCERNING MEDIATION IN PENAL MATTERS

(Adopted by the Committee of Ministers on 15 September 1999 at the 679th meeting of the Ministers' Deputies)

The Committee of Ministers, under the terms of Article 15.*b* of the Statute of the Council of Europe,

Noting the developments in member states in the use of mediation in penal matters as a flexible, comprehensive, problem-solving, participatory option complementary or alternative to traditional criminal proceedings;

Considering the need to enhance active personal participation in criminal proceedings of the victim and the offender and others who may be affected as parties as well as the involvement of the community;

Recognising the legitimate interest of victims to have a stronger voice in dealing with the consequences of their victimisation, to communicate with the offender and to obtain apology and reparation;

Considering the importance of encouraging the offenders' sense of responsibility and offering them practical opportunities to make amends, which may further their reintegration and rehabilitation;

Recognising that mediation may increase awareness of the important role of the individual and the community in preventing and handling crime and resolving its associated conflicts, thus encouraging more constructive and less repressive criminal justice outcomes;

Recognising that mediation requires specific skills and calls for codes of practice and accredited training;

Considering the potentially substantial contribution to be made by non-governmental organisations and local communities in the field of mediation in penal matters and the need to combine and to co-ordinate the efforts of public and private initiatives;

Having regard to the requirements of the Convention for the Protection of Human Rights and Fundamental Freedoms;

Bearing in mind the European Convention on the Exercise of Children's Rights as well as Recommendations No. R (85) 11 on the position of the victim in the framework of criminal law and procedure, No. R (87) 18 concerning the simplification of criminal justice, No. R (87) 21 on assistance to victims and the prevention of victimisation, No. R (87) 20 on social reactions to juvenile delinquency, No. R (88) 6 on social reactions to juvenile delinquency among young people coming from migrant families, No. R (92) 16 on the European Rules on community sanctions and measures, No. R (95) 12 on the management of criminal justice and No. R (98) 1 on family mediation,

Recommends that the governments of member states consider the principles set out in the appendix to this recommendation when developing mediation in penal matters, and give the widest possible circulation to this text.

Appendix to Recommendation No. R (99) 19

I. Definition

These guidelines apply to any process whereby the victim and the offender are enabled, if they freely consent, to participate actively in the resolution of matters arising from the crime through the help of an impartial third party (mediator),

II. General principles

1. Mediation in penal matters should only take place if the parties freely consent. The parties should be able to withdraw such consent at any time during the mediation.

2. Discussions in mediation are confidential and may not be used subsequently, except with the agreement of the parties.

3. Mediation in penal matters should be a generally available service.

4. Mediation in penal matters should be available at all stages of the criminal justice process.

5. Mediation services should be given sufficient autonomy within the criminal justice system.

III. Legal basis

6. Legislation should facilitate mediation in penal matters.

7. There should be guidelines defining the use of mediation in penal matters. Such guidelines should in particular address the conditions for the referral of cases to the mediation service and the handling of cases following mediation.

8. Fundamental procedural safeguards should be applied to mediation; in particular, the parties should have the right to legal assistance and, where necessary, to translation/interpretation. Minors should, in addition, have the right to parental assistance.

IV. The operation of criminal justice in relation to mediation

9. A decision to refer a criminal case to mediation, as well as the assessment of the outcome of a mediation procedure, should be reserved to the criminal justice authorities.

10. Before agreeing to mediation, the parties should be fully informed of their rights, the nature of the mediation process and the possible consequences of their decision.

11. Neither the victim nor the offender should be induced by unfair means to accept mediation.

12. Special regulations and legal safeguards governing minors' participation in legal proceedings should also be applied to their participation in mediation in penal matters.

13. Mediation should not proceed if any of the main parties involved is not capable of understanding the meaning of the process.

14. The basic facts of a case should normally be acknowledged by both parties as a basis for mediation. Participation in mediation should not be used as evidence of admission of guilt in subsequent legal proceedings.

15. Obvious disparities with respect to factors such as the parties' age, maturity or intellectual capacity should be taken into consideration before a case is referred to mediation.

16. A decision to refer a criminal case to mediation should be accompanied by a reasonable time-limit within which the competent criminal justice authorities should be informed of the state of the mediation procedure.

17. Discharges based on mediated agreements should have the same status as judicial decisions or judgments and should preclude prosecution in respect of the same facts (ne bis in idem).

18. When a case is referred back to the criminal justice authorities without an agreement between the parties or after failure to implement such an agreement, the decision as to how to proceed should be taken without delay.

V. The operation of mediation services

V.1. *Standards*

19. Mediation services should be governed by recognised standards.

20. Mediation services should have sufficient autonomy in performing their duties. Standards of competence and ethical rules, as well as procedures for the selection, training and assessment of mediators should be developed.

21. Mediation services should be monitored by a competent body.

V.2. *Qualifications and training of mediators*

22. Mediators should be recruited from all sections of society and should generally possess good understanding of local cultures and communities.

23. Mediators should be able to demonstrate the sound judgment and interpersonal skills necessary to mediation.

24. Mediators should receive initial training before taking up mediation duties as well as in-service training. Their training should aim at providing for a high level of competence, taking into account conflict resolution skills, the specific requirements of working with victims and offenders and basic knowledge of the criminal justice system.

V.3. *Handling of individual cases*

25. Before mediation starts, the mediator should be informed of all relevant facts of the case and be provided with the necessary documents by the competent criminal justice authorities.

26. Mediation should be performed in an impartial manner, based on the facts of the case and on the needs and wishes of the parties. The mediator should always respect the dignity of the parties and ensure that the parties act with respect towards each other.

27. The mediator should be responsible for providing a safe and comfortable environment for the mediation. The mediator should be sensitive to the vulnerability of the parties.

28. Mediation should be carried out efficiently, but at a pace that is manageable for the parties.

29. Mediation should be performed in camera.

30. Notwithstanding the principle of confidentiality, the mediator should convey any information about imminent serious crimes, which may come to light in the course of mediation, to the appropriate authorities or to the persons concerned.

V.4. *Outcome of mediation*

31. Agreements should be arrived at voluntarily by the parties. They should contain only reasonable and proportionate obligations.

32. The mediator should report to the criminal justice authorities on the steps taken and on the outcome of the mediation. The mediator's report should not reveal the contents of mediation sessions, nor express any judgment on the parties' behaviour during mediation.

VI. Continuing development of mediation

33. There should be regular consultation between criminal justice authorities and mediation services to develop common understanding.

34. Member states should promote research on, and evaluation of, mediation in penal matters.

Explanatory memorandum

A. Introduction

I. Background to mediation in penal matters

Towards the end of the twentieth century, a new type of conflict resolution has emerged rivalling the traditional approach of legal settlement. Consensual models of conflict resolution are being propagated as alternatives to the classical pattern of confrontation. This development is not restricted to a particular jurisdiction or a particular branch of the law. Rather, it touches on every legal domain and proliferates in most legal systems.

Consensual models for conflict resolution are not altogether new. The fact, however, that this policy of consensus is no longer a mere theoretical perspective for the distant future, but that it has found its way even into the criminal justice system, with its strong affinities to the state, may indicate that this approach has a strong and widespread appeal. The movement has been variously described as community justice, restorative justice, informal justice etc., but in practice it is most often referred to by means of the technique which most models have in common, which is "mediation" as distinct from legal adjudication.

The mediation movement of today draws support from different ideological sources and strands of thought. It has been stimulated from within as well as without the criminal justice system.

Some elements of negotiation have always existed, of course, within the criminal justice system. Such pragmatic approaches stand in contrast to those positions which, by way of organised mediation programmes, strive for conflict solutions which are more party- and community-oriented, more comprehensive and socially constructive, than traditional criminal procedures. The strength of the movement seems to derive from the fact that its support cuts across ideological and philosophical boundaries. The idea of mediation unites those who want to reconstruct long foregone modes of conflict resolution, those who want to strengthen the position of victims, those who seek alternatives to punishment, and those who want to reduce the expenditure for and workload of the criminal justice system or render this system more effective and efficient.

Models

Mediation in penal matters takes a great many forms. They blend into each other and there are many variations. The major models are as follows.

1. Some form of what could be called "informal mediation" is carried out by criminal justice personnel in the course of their normal work. This might be a public prosecutor who invites the parties to take part in an informal settlement, with the intention of discontinuing prosecution if a satisfactory agreement is reached. It might also be a social worker or probation officer working with a convicted person, who thinks that contact with the victim will make a greater impact on the offender; it might, on the other hand, be a police officer called out to a domestic dispute who may be able to defuse the situation without making a criminal charge. A judge may also choose to attempt an out-of-court settlement and then discharge the case. This kind of informal intervention is common to all legal systems, although the conditions under which it is possible will depend on particular national codes and regulations. Although it is sometimes frequent, it is not systematic or controlled and could be subject to bias and abuse. It also depends on the skills and inclinations of particular personnel and is therefore idiosyncratic. It can be a sensible way of helping the formal system operate more smoothly, but should not be confused with the organised models of mediation which are dealt with in this recommendation.

2. "Traditional village or tribal moots" are long-standing customary arrangements whereby the whole community meets together to resolve conflicts or crimes between its members, still common in less developed countries and rural areas. They depend on very strong integrated communities and are not generally applicable in modern societies. They tend to favour benefit to the community at large. They antedate Western law and have been the inspiration for many modern mediation programmes. The latter are often, in fact, an attempt to introduce the advantages of the tribal moot in a form which is compatible with modern social structures and legally recognised individual rights.

3. When talking of mediation in penal matters, "victim-offender mediation" is the model that people most often have in mind. It involves the immediate parties (although there may be more than one offender or more than one victim) meeting in the presence of a specially appointed mediator (who may be voluntary or paid). The mediation may be performed with both parties present (direct mediation) or if the victim is not willing to meet the offender, in separate meetings with each party (indirect mediation). There are many variants of this model.

In some of these programmes the mediators are criminal justice personnel specially trained to carry out mediation, usually social workers or probation officers, but they may also be police officers, or staff of courts and public prosecutors' offices. In some programmes, independent mediators (professionals or volunteers) without a judicial function are used.

Victim-offender mediation may also be run by a special agency or authority, such as police, youth justice, the probation service, the public prosecutor, court or an independent community-based organisation. In the case of independent programmes, these may be based in organisations involved in victim support or in community-based treatment programmes for offenders, or may be set up specifically to carry out mediation. In some cases, the programme is run by a combination of agencies through an inter-agency steering committee.

This type of mediation may operate at any stage of a case. It may be associated with diversion from prosecution, be in conjunction with a police caution, occur parallel to prosecution, constitute part of a sentence or happen after sentence. An important difference is whether the mediation will or will not affect judicial decisions, as when discontinuation of prosecution depends on an acceptable settlement, or the agreement is put to the court as a recommended order or sentence. The need for control or judicial supervision is much greater if the mediation will have an impact on such decisions.

Some victim-offender mediation programmes apply to any type of offender, whereas others work only with juveniles or with adults, while a few work only with one type of offence, for instance shoplifting, robbery or violence offences. Some programmes are mainly aimed at minor offences or first-time offenders and yet others at more serious offences or even repeat offenders.

4. "Reparation negotiation programmes" exist solely to assess compensation or reparation to be paid by an offender to the victim, usually at the instigation of a court, which will incorporate the reparation in an order. They may involve a mediated meeting between the two parties, but are much more likely to use separate, relatively simple and brief negotiations with each party. Reparation negotiation programmes are not concerned with reconciliation between the parties, but only with the arrangement of material reparation. Some involve work programmes whereby offenders can earn money with which to pay compensation.

5. "Community panels or courts" are programmes which involve the diversion of criminal cases from the prosecution or courts to community procedures that are more flexible and informal, and often involve some element of mediation or negotiation. Local authorities may have their own boards for such mediation.

6. "Family and community group conferences", which have been developed in Australia and New Zealand, represent a further example of community participation in the criminal justice system. They bring together not only the victim and the offender, but also relatives of the offender and other community support persons, certain agencies (such as the police and youth justice) and sometimes support persons for the victim. The offender and his or her family are expected to produce a comprehensive agreement, involving reparation, sanctions and obligations, that is satisfactory to the victim and which they believe will help keep the offender out of further trouble.

Development

In the genealogy of modern mediation programmes, the north American models have acted as trend-setters, although they often incorporate ideas which have been developed elsewhere. Nevertheless, the transatlantic debate prompted the re-emergence of mediation in Europe.

The European development of mediation models is uneven across European countries and in most instances it is still at its initial stages. There is also a wide variety of models existing in various member states. In the United Kingdom, the dominant model has been victim-offender mediation, but there is a large diversity of programmes and models used. The legal constitution of the United Kingdom has allowed extensive involvement of the community.

The continental European scene, which is still developing, is different in that the criminal justice authorities have been more engaged in developing mediation schemes from the outset, and the existing models are often linked to the criminal justice system and reflected in legislation. To mention but a few examples, in Austria, France and Germany there are mediation programmes in penal matters provided for in legislation, according to which criminal cases may be referred to "victim-offender mediation" by the prosecutor, which may result in discontinuation or discharge of the case. In Norway, the mediation boards strive to combine the advantages of mediation with those of a community forum. In practice these boards focus on juveniles. In Spain mediation/reparation programmes for juveniles have been developed by the social authorities within the framework of the criminal justice process. Indeed, the tendency to focus mainly on juveniles has been a prominent feature of mediation programmes across Europe. Often, mediation with juvenile offenders has paved the way for mediation with adults.

Mediation in penal matters is a promising concept which will continue to grow in Europe. Countries with a system in operation are likely to develop it further. In some countries mediation has been introduced recently. Several states are considering the possibility of introducing mediation as a legal option. The ongoing process calls for standards and guidelines in most member states of the Council of Europe.

II. The Council of Europe and mediation

The development of various forms of mediation in several member States has been recognised by the Council of Europe and the need to examine mediation in a European context has been raised on several occasions. In 1998, the Committee of Ministers of the Council of Europe adopted Recommendation No. R(98)1 on family mediation, which highlights the advantages of such mediation and sets out principles for resolving family disputes by way of mediation.

The rise of mediation in penal matters can be retraced by way of examining recent Council of Europe recommendations and reports prepared under the auspices of the European Committee on Crime Problems (CDPC). Although not primarily dealing with mediation, several of the recent recommendations within the field of crime problems concerning, for example, the position of the victim in the framework of criminal law and procedure, assistance to victims and the prevention of victimisation, social reactions to juvenile delinquency and simplification of criminal justice refer to and advocate the use of diversion, conciliation and other forms of out-of-court settlements, such as mediation, in certain situations.

In 1992, the CDPC proposed that a committee of experts on mediation in penal matters, with the objective to evaluate the mounting experience with mediation and to assess its role in relation to the "traditional" criminal justice system, be established. In 1993, the Committee of Ministers endorsed that proposal. Owing to budgetary constraints, the start of the work of the committee was delayed. In the meantime, there were several requests from new member states, as well as observers, to participate in the committee's work. The terms of reference were therefore amended.

The final terms of reference of the Committee of Experts on Mediation in Penal Matters (PC-MP) were adopted by the European Committee on Crime Problems at its 44th plenary session in 1995, and confirmed by the Committee of Ministers at the 543rd meeting of their Deputies in 1995. The terms of reference required the Committee to evaluate different models and programmes of mediation in Europe and to assess the role of mediation in relation to the "traditional" justice system. In particular, the following questions and areas of concern should be studied:

– the potential of mediation to arrive at conflict solutions which are more accepted by those involved (including or excluding society at large) than those solutions which are procured by a traditional criminal procedure;

– the role, training, professional status and degree of professionalisation of mediators;

– the areas of conflict which lend themselves to mediation as well as their underlying problem structure;

– the form and degree of integration into the criminal justice system;

– the relevance and practical implementation of due process requirements in mediation.

The Committee was composed of experts from Austria, Belgium, Bulgaria, Cyprus, the Czech Republic, France, Germany, Greece, Hungary, Ireland, Italy, Liechtenstein, Norway, Slovenia, Spain and Turkey. Representatives of Canada, the European Permanent Conference on Probation and Aftercare (CEP) and the World Society of Victimology, participated as observers. Ms Christa Pelikan (Austria) was elected chair of the committee. The committee included representatives of ministries of justice, the judiciary, prosecution authorities and academics (law, criminology and sociology) as well as persons with practical experience in mediation. Two scientific experts – Mr Heike Jung (Professor of criminal law, Universität des Saarlandes, Germany) and Mr Tony Marshall (former Principal Research Officer, Home Office, United Kingdom) – were appointed to assist the committee. The secretariat was provided by the Directorate of Legal Affairs of the Council of Europe.

The committee held five meetings between November 1996 and April 1999. The members of the committee provided detailed written information on mediation in penal matters in their respective countries. In addition, written information was provided on mediation systems in countries not represented on the Committee. Accordingly, ample information on the legal framework, policy and practice in member states was available to the committee. The text of the draft recommendation and its explanatory memorandum were finalised at the fifth meeting of the Committee of Experts, held in April 1999, and submitted for approval and transmission to the Committee of Ministers at the 48th plenary session of the European Committee on Crime Problems (CDPC), held in June 1999. At the 679th meeting of their Deputies on 15 September 1999, the Committee of Ministers adopted the recommendation and authorised publication of the explanatory memorandum thereto.

B. Commentary on the preamble to the recommendation

The preamble emphasises the benefits of mediation in penal matters. In criminal matters, mediation should be seen as an option which is complementary to traditional criminal proceedings, or even an alternative to them. Thanks to its flexibility and participatory nature, mediation is likely to produce a more comprehensive solution to the problems arising from crime than the criminal justice system can do alone. Seen as an alternative to traditional criminal proceedings and sentencing, mediation also has the potential to reduce the use of custodial sentences and, consequently, the costs of the prison system.

The preamble also reflects the objectives and the philosophy of mediation in penal matters. The involvement of the parties, that is, normally the victim and the offender, as the main actors in a criminal case, is different from that in "traditional" criminal proceedings where the state and the offender are the main actors. One objective of mediation is thus to provide a possibility for the parties to handle their "own" conflict and solve it to their mutual satisfaction. This implies that the parties personally play a more active and constructive, sometimes innovative, role.

Participation in mediation proceedings enables the victim to receive a personal apology and explanation from the offender and to express his or her feelings. This often helps to assuage anger and fear, and thus contributes to greater healing in the long term. Furthermore, in mediation the victim is able to negotiate reparation in a more comprehensive context to suit his or her needs. The victim may thus better understand the offender and his or her behaviour. Some victims may wish to respond to the offender's willingness to accept responsibility by expressing forgiveness.

From the offender perspective, the chance of facing the victim and being able to explain and make an apology is an important element in sensitising the offender to the harm he/she has done and to the pain and suffering he/she has inflicted upon the victim. In addition, through mediation the offender is given the possibility of having direct involvement in resolving the conflict and agreeing reparation (such as financial compensation), which may help to re-establish relations with the community. Thus, the offender's rehabilitation and re-integration into society are promoted by mediation.

Mediation provides a chance to bring the community closer to the criminal justice system by the participation of those who are directly concerned with the crime, by the use of voluntary mediators from the local community, and by the possibility of programmes run by community-based agencies. Community involvement may lead to a better public understanding of crime and consequently encourage community support for victims, rehabilitation of offenders and prevention of crime.

Mediation therefore shows that satisfying the interests of the victim, the offender and society at large are not incompatible. Socially constructive solutions are of benefit to all parties concerned. The conciliatory nature of mediation can assist the criminal justice system in fulfilling one of its fundamental objectives, namely contributing to a peaceful and safe society, by restoring balance and social peace after a crime has been committed.

The diversity and mix of public and private programmes in the field of mediation calls for co-ordination and co-operation supported by common standards. Mediation practices have accumulated a body of knowledge distinct from other practices related to criminal justice. But mediation must not be approached lightly. Mediators need training and experience in the use of specific skills. While mediation involves flexibility and diversity of action, its underlying principles should be enshrined in codes of practice. This would help ensure quality of service and credibility of mediation as such.

The reference to the European Convention on Human Rights in the preamble emphasises the relevance of the protection of individuals' fundamental rights. Mediation introduces a greater degree of flexibility into the criminal justice system. In some instances this may create a risk of overlooking or disregarding some of the current rules protecting individual rights. Mediation therefore needs to be accompanied by a number of safeguards as they are spelled out in the European Convention on Human Rights.

Furthermore, the preamble refers to other instruments of the Council of Europe, which in certain situations make reference to the use of mediation and similar schemes. Thus:

– the European Convention on the Exercise of Children's Rights requires, in its Article 13, the contracting parties to encourage the institutionalisation and the use of mediation procedures;

– Recommendation No. R(85)11 on the position of the victim in the framework of criminal law and procedure recommends member states to examine the possible advantages of mediation and conciliation schemes;

– Recommendation No. R(87)18 concerning the simplification of criminal justice recommends member states to review their legislation to promote out-of-court settlements;

– Recommendation No. R(87)20 on social reactions to juvenile delinquency calls on governments to review their legislation and practice with a view to encouraging the development of diversion and mediation procedures;

– Recommendation No. R(87)21 on assistance to victims and the prevention of victimisation recommends that member states encourage experiments (whether on a national or a local basis) in mediation between offenders and victims;

- Recommendation No. (92) 16 on the European rules on community sanctions and measures refers to measures which maintain the offender in the community through obligations alternative to deprivation of liberty (for example, mediation);

- Recommendation No. (92) 17 concerning consistency in sentencing underlines that sentencing rationale in member states should be consistent with modern and humane crime policies in particular with respect to reducing the use of imprisonment by, inter alia, using measures of diversion such as mediation. It also considers the importance of ensuring the compensation of victims;

- Recommendation No. R (95) 12 on the management of criminal justice recalls that crime policies such as decriminalisation, depenalisation or diversion, mediation and the simplification of criminal procedure can contribute to addressing difficulties of criminal justice systems such as an increase in workloads and budgetary constraints;

- Recommendation No. R (98) 1 seeks to promote family mediation.

It should be emphasised that the principles contained in the recommendation, although sometimes rather elaborate, should be seen as providing guidance and a source of inspiration when developing domestic systems of mediation in penal matters. It is clear that a considerable margin of appreciation must be left to member states in order to make such mediation fit the legal tradition in each member state.

C. Commentary on the appendix

I. Definition

As a term of reference, "mediation" needs explanation. This has to do with the fact that various other terms are being used to describe programmes or approaches which, like mediation, aim at consensus. On the one hand, precision in definition is wanted. On the other hand, such a definition should take into account the existing diversity of programmes and models.

It helps to know that in France, for example, the term *"médiation"* is, in the context of legal processes, reserved, in principle, for the domain of the adult criminal justice system, whereas the term *"réparation"* describes similar practices in juvenile criminal justice. In Germany, discussion has been centred on the term *"Täter-Opfer-Ausgleich"* and, in Austria, the term *"Außergerichtlicher Tatausgleich"* is being used. The Norwegian model refers to *"konflikt* and *mediation"*. In the United Kingdom "mediation" and "reparation" were originally used interchangeably and there is a growing tendency to refer more generally to "restorative justice". Such differences in terminology hint at differences in the genesis, objective and framework of mediation programmes.

The term "mediation" in a general sense (that is, not specific to a penal context) is normally reserved for a process of conflict resolution, involving intervention by an impartial third party with the intention of encouraging voluntary agreement between the parties.

In the recommendation, mediation in penal matters is defined as a process whereby the victim and the offender[1] can be enabled, voluntarily, to participate actively in the resolution of matters arising from the crime through the help of an impartial third party or mediator. The reference only to the victim and the offender as parties does not exclude other persons (legal and physical) participating in the mediation.

Such an approach may take various forms, and they are often combined with each other, for instance:

- a sharing of views so that victim and offender understand each other better;
- an apology and voluntary agreement for the offender to make reparation to the victim;
- a voluntary agreement by the offender to undertake some other action, such as work for the community or participation in a rehabilitation programme ("indirect reparation");
- the resolution of any conflict between the victim and offender, or between their families or friends;
- a programme of agreed sanctions and undertakings which may be placed before a court as a suggested sentence or court order.

Mediation in penal matters may operate in direct or indirect forms, that is, with the parties meeting together or being seen separately by the mediator. It may be carried out by professional mediators or by trained lay volunteers. Mediation may be carried out under the auspices of a criminal justice agency or an independent community-based organisation. The parties may be a victim and an offender (as in "classic" victim/offender mediation), or they may include their relatives, other community supporters and representatives of criminal justice agencies (as in the "family or community group conferences"). In all circumstances, it is essential that the mediator is impartial and that participation is voluntary.

II. General principles

The general principles reflect the essential elements for mediation in penal matters. They clarify the important place of mediation within the criminal justice system, the main characteristics of mediation (voluntary participation and confidentiality) as well as its availability as a service to victims and offenders.

1. Since mediation has no chance of succeeding unless the parties are willing to participate, voluntary participation is a prerequisite for all forms of mediation. This distinguishes mediation from traditional criminal justice proceedings and

---

[1]. The term "offender" which is, for practical reasons, used throughout the recommendation and the explanatory memorandum would also cover the alleged offender, for example, the accused or any person charged with a criminal offence.

indicates that the parties in mediation "own" their case to a large extent. Free consent must be given at the outset. Parties may withdraw their consent at any time. The criminal justice authorities and the mediator should make this clear to the parties before and at the beginning of the mediation respectively.

2. Mediation in penal matters cannot do without respecting the principle of confidentiality for two main reasons. On the one hand, it is a prerequisite for a fruitful exchange and constructive outcome. It facilitates an environment where the parties can safely bring in more aspects than may be advisable in traditional court proceedings. Such additional information is often the basis for reaching an out-of-court settlement. On the other hand, confidentiality protects the interests of the parties. The discussion during mediation should therefore not be made public, unless the parties agree. This stands in contrast with the requirement of a public hearing in traditional criminal proceedings and emphasises the "private character" of mediation. Confidentiality applies not only vis-à-vis the general public but also in relation to the criminal justice system. An exception from the principle of confidentiality is recognised in paragraph 30.

3. Up to now mediation has been managed on a rudimentary basis in many member states. In some countries it has become a more or less comprehensive service. It is important that the services are fully comprehensive for reasons of equality of access and quality of service. Therefore, the recommendation calls on member states to promote mediation programmes, public or private, as a generally available service. This would, as a minimum, imply that mediation – whether public or private programmes – would be officially recognised by the states as a possibility, alternative or complementary to traditional criminal proceedings. Such programmes should normally have funding from a public budget (state and/or municipality) and there should normally be some kind of public accountability. The recommendation does not go so far as to characterise mediation as a "right" however. It should be seen as a legal option which should be considered by the criminal justice authorities.

4. Mediation can be used at different stages of the criminal process. The availability of mediation at different stages varies considerably from country to country. While many programmes operate at any stage, others may be entirely associated with diversion from prosecution (conditional or otherwise), be in conjunction with a police caution, occur parallel to prosecution, constitute part of a sentence (for example, an order to make reparation), or happen after sentencing. It is recommended that mediation be available throughout the whole criminal justice process. This takes into account that the parties (particularly the victim) may not be ready to take advantage of mediation at an early stage. However, in many cases it is important to settle matters as soon as possible.

5. The autonomy of mediation services within the criminal justice system ensures that the mediation process operates on the basis of a different rationale from the "traditional" criminal justice system. Mediation services need sufficient autonomy to act flexibly and responsibly towards the parties.

Of course, mediation services cannot operate as if they were totally detached from the criminal justice system. Criminal justice agencies should have sufficient authority to perform their "gate-keeping" role and their ultimate responsibility for the legality of the process. This involves the assessment of issues of public interest and procedural rights and safeguards of the parties when making decisions both before and after mediation. In addition, there are individual rights that must be protected during mediation, which implies that the criminal justice authorities need to ensure monitoring of mediation practices.

III. Legal basis

6. With a view to avoiding over-regulating mediation and considering the various approaches to mediation in member states, the recommendation does not explicitly require that mediation programmes should be laid down in law. Legislation should, however, as a minimum rule, make mediation possible and even facilitate its use.

Procedural rights and safeguards

Procedural rights and safeguards have to be taken into account during mediation. The extent, to which this should be laid down in law may depend on the legal tradition of the particular member state.

Mediation is of a less formal character than criminal proceedings are, in order to allow for a more personal and comprehensive approach to conflict resolution. This cannot, and should not, be regulated in detail. Yet, there are procedural rights and safeguards of the individuals in the criminal process which cannot be dispensed with in a society governed by the rule of law. Mediation, as an integral part of the criminal process, should therefore receive legal recognition and operate in conformity with the fundamental rights of the persons involved. The relevant regulation, in this respect, is, in particular, Article 6 of the European Convention on Human Rights (ECHR) on the right to a fair trial, which reads:

> "1. In the determination of his civil rights and obligations or of any criminal charge against him, everyone is entitled to a fair and public hearing within a reasonable time by an independent and impartial tribunal established by law. Judgment shall be pronounced publicly but the press and public may be excluded from all or part of the trial in the interests of morals, public order or national security in a democratic society, where the interests of juveniles or the protection of the private life of the parties so require, or to the extent strictly necessary in the opinion of the court in special circumstances where publicity would prejudice the interests of justice.
>
> 2. Everyone charged with a criminal offence shall be presumed innocent until proved guilty according to law.
>
> 3. Everyone charged with a criminal offence has the following minimum rights:
>
> *a.* to be informed promptly, in a language which he understands and in detail, of the nature and cause of the accusation against him;

    b. to have adequate time and facilities for the preparation of his defence;

    c. to defend himself in person or through legal assistance of his own choosing or, if he has not sufficient means to pay for legal assistance, to be given it free when the interests of justice so require;

    d. to examine or have examined witnesses against him and to obtain the attendance and examination of witnesses on his behalf under the same conditions as witnesses against him;

    e. to have the free assistance of an interpreter if he cannot understand or speak the language used in court."

It follows that Article 6 of the European Convention on Human Rights applies to all cases where a criminal charge is at stake. In principle, cases of mediation originating in a criminal charge would thus be covered. To what extent the various rights under Article 6 apply when mediation is used as an alternative to traditional criminal justice proceedings needs to be discussed in more detail .

The right of access to a court (Article 6.1)

According to the "Deweer case" (European Court of Human Rights, Judgment of 27 February 1980, Series A, No. 35) "the right to a court" (Article 6.1) is no more absolute in criminal than in civil matters and it could be subject to implied limitations, for example, a decision not to prosecute. Furthermore, according to the same judgment, such a right could be waived by the parties, as long as a high degree of vigilance is provided for such a waiver. Agreeing to mediation, in the context of a diversion procedure, may constitute a waiver of the "right of access to a court". The crucial consideration would thus be whether the waiver was made under proper circumstances.

The recommendation therefore makes a distinction between "the operation of criminal justice in relation to mediation" (Section IV) and "the operation of mediation services" (Section V). That distinction is also reflected in the "legal basis" of mediation, paragraphs 7 and 8.

7.   This paragraph concerns the criminal justice authorities which need to have guidelines indicating when mediation may be used. Such guidelines may indicate types of offences suitable for mediation or conditions related to the parties. It is, for example, necessary that the accused accepts relevant facts of the case. He or she may generally have to admit a degree of responsibility falling short of recognising criminal liability. Due to the principle of presumption of innocence, Article 6.2 ECHR, no decision on guilt may be taken by the criminal justice authorities without proper court proceedings, that is, in compliance with Article 6. Domestic regulation should therefore focus on factual conditions of a case and safeguards for the parties, before and during the referral. The main considerations are listed in Section IV.

8.   As to the operation of mediation provided by the mediation services, it is recommended that certain fundamental rights which apply during mediation should

be explicitly regulated. Primary amongst these is the right to legal counselling/assistance, translation/interpretation and parental assistance (or, if need be, assistance by other representatives) for minors.

IV. The operation of criminal justice in relation to mediation

This section of the recommendation relates to the role of the criminal justice authorities and provides guidelines for their "gate-keeping" function.

9. Mediation in criminal cases should be dependent on a decision by the criminal justice authorities (normally the prosecution or the court). A "criminal case" would be at stake as soon as the crime has been reported to the police. The assessment of a mediation process, once it is finished, should also be reserved to the criminal justice authorities (cf. General Principles, paragraph 5).

10. It is crucial that parties, before agreeing to mediation, are fully aware of their "procedural situation", based on the facts of the case. They should also have the right to a comprehensive explanation of how the mediation procedure is going to be performed, by what service or by whom, and its possible consequences, in terms of criminal justice decisions, of the different outcomes of mediation (for example, success, failure or partial settlement). The burden of information lies with the criminal justice authorities. Each party should be informed separately, if need be. Such information is necessary for the parties to be able to exercise informed consent, in conformity with paragraph 1.

11. Bearing in mind the general principle contained in paragraph 1, it is of the utmost importance that the consent to mediation by the parties is not reached by "unfair means". The criminal justice authorities must make sure that the information given to the parties, referred to in paragraph 10, is objectively presented. They may not use any pressure on the parties in order to make them agree to mediation, and they should ensure that one party does not induce the other to agree to mediation by threats, and so on. In short, the criminal justice authorities must make sure that no form of improper constraint influences the parties' agreement to mediation.

12. Special domestic regulations and legal safeguards that apply to minors in traditional criminal proceedings shall also apply to the process of referral of a case to mediation as well as during mediation. This rule implies a special monitoring function by the criminal justice authorities over the mediation procedure where minors are involved. The legal safeguards should in particular cover the rights to receive information, to express his or her views, to have a representative (parental or other), and to a speedy procedure. The criminal justice authorities must always consider the procedural issues, as well as the mediation as such with the best interest of the child in mind (see the United Nations Convention on the Rights of the Child and the European Convention on the Exercise of Children's Rights).

13. This rule excludes mediation in cases where one of the main parties is unable to comprehend the mediation process on intellectual grounds. These may be due to age or mental retardation, or a similar handicap. The reference to the "main parties" implies that cases involving more than two parties may still be referred to

mediation, even if one of the parties would not understand the process, provided that party only plays a minor role.

14. It is a normal requirement for mediation that the victim, as well as the accused, accept the relevant main facts of the case. Without such a common understanding, the possibility of reaching an agreement during mediation is limited, if not excluded. It is not necessary that the accused, in addition, accept guilt, and the criminal justice authorities may not pre-judge the question of guilt in order not to infringe the principle of the presumption of innocence (Article 6.2 ECHR). It is sufficient that the accused admits some responsibility for what has happened. Furthermore, it is emphasised that participation in mediation should not be used against the accused if the case is referred back to the criminal justice authorities after mediation. Moreover, an acceptance of facts or even "confession of guilt" by the accused, in the context of mediation, should not be used as evidence in subsequent criminal proceedings on the same matter.

15. Mediation may not be an appropriate procedure where there are obvious discrepancies between the parties. Mediation requires active participation by the parties and an ability to take decisions in their own interest in the course of negotiation. Large power imbalances, such as a relationship of dependency by one party on another, implicit or explicit threats of violence, would prevent free participation and true consent to agreement. It should be recognised, however, that many discrepancies in power and skills can be corrected by mediators who will seek to redress the balance in favour of disadvantaged parties.

16. The phenomenon of lengthy criminal proceedings is an acknowledged problem in several member states. Mediation has to be conducted at a pace which is comfortable for the parties. The time-limit specified in this rule ensures that the criminal justice authorities receive the necessary feed-back to make proper decisions within a reasonable time. If mediation has not been completed by this time-limit, the criminal justice authorities have to consider whether or not to resume normal criminal proceedings in conformity with the "celerity principle". (This would not always mean that the mediation cannot continue, on a private basis, if the parties so desire and are still in a position to do so; see also paragraph 28).

17. This rule applies when a case has been mediated successfully, the criminal justice authorities accept the result and, as a consequence, the criminal proceedings are brought to an end (order not to prosecute or for the discontinuance of the proceedings). Such a decision by the criminal justice authorities should make it impossible that the case (the same facts) be brought up again (ne bis in idem), provided that the agreement is implemented and that the decision has acquired legal force.

18. If mediation is unsuccessful in bringing about an agreement between the parties, or where an agreement is reached but not complied with by the parties, the criminal justice authorities normally proceed with their proceedings. In accordance with paragraph 16, lengthy proceedings should be avoided: the continuation of the case should be decided without delay.

V. The operation of mediation services

This section deals with the handling of mediation once a criminal case has been referred to mediation and the case is thus no longer under the immediate control of the criminal justice system. This section also provides general guidelines for mediation in cases not originating in the criminal justice system.

V.1. *Standards*

19. The recommendation reflects the view that mediation should be regulated only to the extent necessary and that mediation services should be given independence and autonomy in performing their duties. However, considering that it is recommended that mediation should be a generally available service, there is a need for some standard-setting concerning the organisation of mediation services as well as for the operation of mediation. Such standards should preferably be recognised by the state, municipality or other body of public character. It is not necessary that they be made into law or regulations. However, some kind of official recognition would be preferable.

20. Within the framework described in paragraphs 19 and 21, the mediation service should have sufficient autonomy to develop standards concerning qualifications of the personnel, codes of conduct and/or ethical codes for performing mediation. It is also recommended that procedures for recruitment of mediators and systems for evaluating their performance be developed. Such measures would provide for a necessary degree of professionalism of the service.

21. In the light of its recognised standards, the mediation service should be monitored by an independent organ. This monitoring could be performed by the criminal justice authorities. However, the recommendation only refers to "a competent body" which does not exclude other authorities.

V.2. *Qualifications and training of mediators*

The recommendation, in respect of qualification and training, only specifies a minimum level of requirements referring to the background and personal skills of a potential mediator and the objectives of the training. Member states would be expected to develop more extensive standards and guidelines (such standards already exist in a few member states).

22. Mediators (professionals or volunteers) should, as far as possible, represent all sections of society in the areas where they are supposed to work. In particular, they should be recruited from all social groups, including ethnic and minority groups. Both sexes should be represented. The mediators should preferably possess a good all-round knowledge, in particular concerning the local environment in which they are active. Education and qualifications are not necessarily the most important elements in selecting mediators. The recommendation makes no reference to minimum age, although provision to that effect may be appropriate at national level.

23. As to the personal skills of mediators, the recommendation mentions "sound judgment", which would normally be related to a high degree of maturity. "Interpersonal skills" necessary to mediation would, for instance, include an open attitude towards people, ability to listen and to communicate, and to remain impartial. Such abilities should be reflected in selection and training procedures.

24. All mediators need a minimum level of initial training, and their training should continue throughout the course of their work. The contents of their training should be linked to the standards of the mediation service. Such training should aim at developing the specific skills and techniques needed for conflict resolution. In addition, the training should provide for a good understanding of the general problems of victims and victimisation which, for example, can be obtained from victim support groups, as well as problems concerning offenders and related social problems. The institutionalisation of training would not only be beneficial for mediators in their work; it would also contribute to higher standards of mediation.

V.3. *Handling of individual cases*

25. At the outset of the mediation, the mediator needs an adequate picture of the factual circumstances of the case. This information, provided by the criminal justice authorities, is necessary, in the first place, to define precisely the offence to which the mediation is related, and secondly, to assist the mediator in assessing whether the case is suitable for mediation. Additional information concerning the parties, which is relevant to decisions on mediation, should be submitted to the extent necessary and possible, according to domestic legislation, if the parties agree.

26. Mediation should be performed in an impartial manner. This implies that the mediator does not take sides but seeks to help the parties to participate fully and derive benefit from mediation. Impartiality also implies that the mediator does not appear to be partial from the perspective of the parties because of personal links with one of the parties or previous involvement in the case. Accordingly, a person should not be appointed mediator if he/she has personal links with the parties or if he/she is personally involved in the case. The emphasis on impartiality does not in principle exclude criminal justice personnel from performing mediation. However, the prosecutor in charge of a case should not act as a mediator in the same matter.

The requirement of impartiality does not imply that the mediator should be indifferent to the fact that the offence has been committed and the wrongdoing of the offender. The parties of mediation in penal matters are, thus, unlike parties in mediation in civil matters, initially unequal with the main obligations resting on the offender's side. However, in relation to the principle of the presumption of innocence, the mediator must take no position on the question of guilt.

27. This rule implies a responsibility for the mediator to ensure that the place of mediation is chosen in the interests of the parties, that is, normally a neutral place. The meeting should be controlled in such a way that the parties remain respectful of each other and are able to feel safe and comfortable. The vulnerability of the

parties should be carefully considered in that context. If the requirements of this paragraph cannot be satisfied, the case is not suited to mediation. In such a situation mediation should be ended and the case referred back to the criminal justice authorities.

28. Mediation, as an integral part of the criminal justice process, should be carried out efficiently. As one of the arguments for introducing mediation in penal matters is to increase efficiency of the system, mediation should proceed with all due speed within the limits set by the capacities and wishes of the parties.

29. This paragraph, which specifies the principle of confidentiality (see also General principles, paragraph 2), suggests that mediation sessions, as a rule, should not be open to the public, the objective being that of providing confidence between the parties and the mediator (see also paragraph 32).

30. In case of imminent serious crime, a balance must be struck between the principle of confidentiality (General principles, paragraph 2) and the need to prevent serious harm or damage. Therefore, the principle of confidentiality does not extend to imminent serious crime that may be revealed during mediation. In such a case, the mediator should inform the proper authorities, which will often, but need not necessarily, be the criminal justice authorities. In some cases it may be advisable to inform the persons concerned. Like other citizens the mediator, in such cases, should have an obligation to comply with the requirements of domestic law pertaining to the reporting and prevention of such crimes.

V.4. *Outcome of mediation*

31. There are three main requirements for an agreement after mediation: it should be voluntary, reasonable and proportionate.

The requirement that agreements through mediation should be completely voluntary is absolute. This distinguishes mediation from adjudication and arbitration, where an impartial person listens to the parties and may encourage greater informality and flexibility than the courts, but comes up with his or her own decision. The requirement that agreements should be voluntary does not exclude the mediator, however, from playing an active role in reaching the agreement.

The requirement of a reasonable obligation implies some relationship between the offence and the type of obligation on the offender.

The proportionality requirement means that, within rather wide limits, there should be correspondence between the burden on the offender and the seriousness of the offence; for instance, compensation should not be excessive.

32. After the mediation process is concluded, the mediator should report to the criminal justice authorities on the procedural steps taken during mediation and on the outcome. In the case of an unsuccessful outcome, the report should, if possible, indicate briefly the reasons. However, according to the principle of confidentiality, the report should not reveal the contents of statements and behaviour of the parties during mediation. The report should preferably be in written form, ideally following a standard formula.

VI. Continuing development of mediation

33. Mediation is a relatively new phenomenon in most European countries. It needs wide acceptance by society at large as well as by the criminal justice system with which it will work closely. Common understanding and mutual respect are of the utmost importance. In particular, there is a need to show that mediation brings additional qualities to the criminal justice procedure, and the mediation services must be able to demonstrate a high level of competence. In order to achieve this, regular contacts and consultations between members of the mediation services and members of the criminal justice system (including ministries of justice, courts, prosecution and police) should be encouraged.

34. Closely linked to the recommendation in paragraph 33 is that concerning research and evaluation. Research is concerned, inter alia, with procedures of objective description and assessment. Research is essential for gaining knowledge on the functioning of mediation. Without such knowledge, there is no trustworthy basis for describing and assessing the extent to which such measures are being used and their results. For the further development of mediation, the evaluation of existing models is essential. There is a need for evaluative research on mediation in penal matters, in particular as it is still in its initial stages in most European countries. The present paragraph, therefore, encourages the promotion of such research.

REFERENCES

Aaltonen, A. (n.d.), *Mediated case – mediated price. A cost-effect comparison of mediation and court procedures*, unpublished report (English summary).

Aertsen, I. and Peters, T. (1998), "Mediation for Reparation: The Victim's Perspective", *European Journal of Crime, Criminal Law and Criminal Justice*, vol. 6/2, 106-124.

Aertsen, I., Vanfraechem, I. and Willemsens, J. (eds.) (2004), *Restorative Justice in Europe: Empirical Research*, Leuven, Leuven University Press.

Akester, K. (2000), *Restoring youth justice: new directions in domestic and international law and practice, Justice*, 59 Carter Lane, London EC4 V 5 AQ, admin@justice.org.uk.

Altweger, A. and Hitzl, E. (2001), *Kundenzufriedenheit der Geschädigten im Außergerichtlichen Tatausgleich*, Diploma thesis, Innsbruck.

Baldry, A.C., De Leo, G. and Scardaccione, G. (1998), "Victim/offender mediation in the Italian juvenile justice system: a first attempt at definition", in Boros, J., Munich, I. and Szegedi, M. (eds.), *Psychology and criminal justice: international review of theory and practice*, Berlin, Walter de Gruyter.

Bogensberger, W. (1994), "Gleiches (Straf-)Recht für alle", in Hammerschick, W., Pelikan, C. and Pilgram, A. (eds.), *Ausweg aus dem Strafrecht – der Außergerichtliche Tatausgleich*, Baden-Baden, Nomos, 179-190.

Bonafé-Schmitt, J.-P. (1992), *La médiation; une justice douce*, Paris, Syros-Alternatives.

Braithwaite, J. (2002), *Restorative justice and responsive regulation*, New York, Oxford University Press.

Christie, N. (1977), "Conflicts as property", *British Journal of Criminology*, 17(1), 1-15.

Daly, K. (2003), "Mind the gap: restorative justice in theory and practice" in von Hirsch, A., Roberts, J., Bottoms, A.E., Roach, K. and Schiff, M. (eds.), *Restorative justice and criminal justice: competing or reconcilable paradigms?*, Oxford, Hart Publishing, 219-236.

Dignan, J. (2004), "Empirical research with regard to restorative justice in England and Wales" in Aertsen, I., Vanfraechem, I. and Willemsens, J. (eds.), *Restorative Justice in Europe: Empirical Research*, Leuven, Leuven University Press.

Dignan, J. and Marsh, P. (2001), "Restorative justice and family group conferences in England: current state and future prospects", in Morris, A. and Maxwell, G. (eds.), *Restorative justice for juveniles: conferencing, mediation and circles*, Oxford, Hart Publishing, 85-101.

Dölling, D. and Henninger, S. (1998), "Sonstige empirische Untersuchungen zum TOA", in Dolling, D. et al., *Täter-Opfer-Ausgleich in Deutschland*, Bonn, Bundesministerium der Justiz, 203-371.

European Forum for Victim-Offender Mediation and Restorative Justice (ed.) (2000), *Victim-offender mediation in Europe: making restorative justice work*, Leuven, Leuven University Press.

Gimenez-Salinas, E. (1997), "La mediación en el sistema de justicia juvenil: una visión desde el derecho comparado", *Annales Internationales de Criminologie*, 35-1/2, 155-176.

Groenhuijsen, M. (2000), "Victim-offender mediation: legal and procedural safeguards. Experiments and legislation in some European jurisdictions", in European Forum for Victim-Offender Mediation and Restorative Justice (ed.), *Victim-Offender Mediation in Europe. Making Restorative Justice Work*, Leuven, Leuven University Press, 69-81.

Hadley, M.J. (ed.) (2001), *The spiritual roots of restorative justice*, Albany, NY, State University of New York Press.

Hammerschick, W., Pelikan, C. and Pilgram, A. (1994), *Ausweg aus dem Strafrecht – der Außergerichtliche Tatausgleich*, Baden-Baden, Nomos.

Hartmann, A. (1995), *Schlichten oder Richten: das Täter-Opfer-Ausgleich und das (Jugend-)Strafrecht*, Munich, Fink.

Home Office (2003), *Restorative justice: the Government's strategy*, London, Home Office Communications Directorate.

International Network For Research on Restorative Justice for Juveniles (1997), "Declaration of Leuven on the advisability of promoting the restorative approach to juvenile crime; made on the occasion of the first International Conference on "Restorative Justice for Juveniles. Potentialities, Risks and Problems for Research", Leuven, May 12-14, 1997, *European Journal on Criminal Policy and Research*, 5.4, 118-122.

Jullion, D. (2000), "Victim-Offender Mediation in France", in European Forum for Victim-Offender Mediation and Restorative Justice (ed.), *Victim-Offender Mediation in Europe. Making Restorative Justice Work,* Leuven, Leuven University Press, 211-249.

Kerner, H.-J., Hartmann, A. and Lenz, S. (2003), *Täter-Opfer Ausgleich in der Entwicklung. Auswertung der bundesweiten Täter-Opfer-Ausgleich-Statistik für die Jahre 1993 bis 2001*, Tübingen, Institut für Kriminologie.

Kilchling, M. and Kaiser, M. (1996) in Greer, D. (ed.), *Compensating Crime Victims. A European Survey*, edition iuscrim, Contributions and Materials from the Max Planck Institute for Foreign and International Criminal Law, Vol. S 59, Freiburg i. Br., 255-297.

Killias, M. et al. (2003), *European Sourcebook of Crime and Criminal Justice Statistics – 2003*, Meppel, Boom Juridische Uitgevers.

Kurki, L. (2003), "Evaluating restorative justice practices", in von Hirsch, A., Roberts, J., Bottoms, A.E., Roach, K. and Schiff, M. (eds.), *Restorative justice and criminal justice: competing or reconcilable paradigms?*, Oxford, Hart Publishing, 293-314.

Latimer, J., Dowden, C., Muise, D. (2001), *The effectiveness of restorative justice practices: a meta-analysis*, Research and Statistics Division, Department of Justice Canada.

Launay, G. and Murray, P. (1989), "Victim/offender groups", in Wright, M. and Galaway, B. (eds.), *Mediation and Criminal Justice. Victims, Offenders and Community*, London, Sage Publications, 113-131.

Lauwaert, K. and Aertsen, I. (2002), "Restorative justice: activities and expectations at European level", *ERA Forum: scripta iuris europaei*, (1), 27-32.

Lee, A. (1996), "Public Attitudes Towards Restorative Justice", in Galaway, B. and Hudson, J. (eds.), *Restorative Justice: International Perspectives*, Monsey, Criminal Justice Press, 337-347.

Lilles, H. (2001), "Circle sentencing: part of the restorative justice continuum", in Morris, A. and Maxwell, G., R*estorative justice for juveniles: conferencing, mediation and circles*, Oxford, Hart, 161-179.

Löschnig-Gspandl, M. and Kilchling, M. (1997), "Victim/Offender Mediation and Victim Compensation in Austria and Germany – Stocktaking and Perspectives for Future Research", *European Journal of Crime, Criminal Law and Criminal Justice*, 5/1, 58-78.

Mackay, R.E. (2000), "Ethics and Good Practice in Restorative Justice", in European Forum for Victim-Offender Mediation and Restorative Justice (ed.), *Victim-Offender Mediation in Europe. Making Restorative Justice Work*, Leuven, Leuven University Press, 49-67.

Mackay, R.E. (1996), "Victimology and Rights Theories", *International Review of Victimology*, 4/3, 183-194.

Maguire, M. and Corbett, C. (1987), *The effects of crime and the work of Victim Support schemes*, Gower, Aldershot.

Marshall, T.F. (1999), *Restorative Justice. An Overview*, London, Home Office.

Marshall, T. (1996), "The evolution of restorative justice in Britain", *European Journal on Criminal Policy and Research*, 4.4, 21-43.

Mattinson, J. and Mirrlees-Black, C. (2000), *Attitudes to crime and criminal justice: findings from the 1998 British Crime Survey*, London, Home Office.

Maxwell, G. and Morris, A. (2001), "Family group conferences and reoffending", in Morris, A. and Maxwell, G. (eds.), *Restorative justice for juveniles: conferencing, mediation and circles*, Oxford, Hart Publishing, 243-263.

Mayhew, P. and van Kesteren, J. (2002), "Cross-national attitudes to punishment", in Roberts, J.V. and Hough, M. (eds.), *Changing attitudes to punishment: public opinion, crime and justice*, Cullompton, Willan Publishing, 63-92.

McCold, P. (2003), "A survey of assessment research on mediation and conferencing" in Walgrave, L. (ed.), *Repositioning restorative justice*, Cullompton, Willan Publishing, 67-120.

McCold, P. and Wachtel, T. (2002), "Restorative justice theory validation", in Weitekamp, E. and Kerner, H.-J. (eds.), *Restorative Justice. Theoretical foundations*, Cullompton, Willan Publishing, 110-142.

McElrea, F.W.M. (1998), *The New Zealand model of family group conferences*, Paper to international symposium "Beyond prisons: best practices along the criminal justice process", March 18, 1998, Kingston, Ontario, Canada.

Mediation UK (2003), *40 cases: restorative justice and victim/offender mediation*, ed. by Crosland, P. and Liebmann, M., Bristol, Mediation UK, www.mediationuk.org.uk.

Ministry of Justice New Zealand (1995), *Restorative Justice. A discussion paper*, Wellington, Ministry of Justice.

Morris, A. and Maxwell, G. (2003), "Restorative justice in New Zealand", in von Hirsch, A., Roberts, J., Bottoms, A.E., Roach, K. and Schiff, M. (eds.), *Restorative justice and criminal justice: competing or reconcilable paradigms?*, Oxford, Hart Publishing, 257-271.

Morris, A. and Maxwell, G. (eds.) (2001), *Restorative justice for juveniles: conferencing, mediation and circles*, Oxford, Hart Publishing.

Newburn, T. et al. (2001), *The introduction of referral orders into the youth justice system: second interim report*, RDS Occasional Paper 73, London, Home Office.

Novack, S., Galaway, B. and Hudson, J. (1980), "Victim and Offender Perceptions in the Fairness of Restitution and Community-Service Sanctions", in Hudson, J. and Galaway, J. (eds.), *Victims, Offenders and Alternative Sanctions*, Lexington, D.C. Heath and Company, 63-70.

Reeves, H. (1989), "The Victim Support Perspective", in Wright, M. and Galaway, B. (eds.), *Mediation and Criminal Justice. Victims, Offenders and Community*, London, SAGE Publications, 44-55.

Restorative Justice Consortium (1998), *Standards for restorative justice*, London, the RJC.

Restorative Justice Consortium (UK), *Principles of Restorative Justice* (http://www.restorativejustice.org.uk)

Roberts, J.V. and Hough, M. (eds.) (2002), *Changing attitudes to punishment: public opinion, crime and justice*, Cullompton, Willan Publishing.

Roche, D. (2003), *Accountability in restorative justice*, Oxford, Oxford University Press.

Schafer, S. (1960), *Restitution to victims of crime*, London, Stevens.

Schüler-Springorum, H. (1991), *Kriminalpolitik fuer Menschen*, Frankfurt, Suhrkamp.

Schütz, H. (1999), "Die Rückfallhäufigkeit nach einem Außergerichtlichen Tatausgleich bei Erwachsenen", *Österreichische Richterzeitung*, 161-166.

Sessar, K. (1992), *Wiedergutmachen oder strafen. Einstellungen in der Bevölkerung und in der Justiz*, Pffenweiler, Centaurus-Verlag.

Shapland, J., Wilmore, J. and Duff, P. (1985), *Victims in the Criminal Justice System*, Aldershot, Gower Publishing.

Sherman, L.W. and Strang, H. (1997), *Restorative Justice and Deterring Crime*, Reintegrative Shaming Experiments (RISE), Australian National University, Canberra, RISE Working Papers: Paper No. 4.

Stevens, J. (2000), *Access to justice in sub-Saharan Africa: the role of traditional and informal justice systems*, London, Penal Reform International.

Strang, H. (2002), *Repair or revenge: victims and restorative justice*, Oxford, Clarendon.

Trujillo, M.F.J. (2000), *Mediation: would it work in Spain too?*, Unpublished dissertation, Master of European Criminology, Catholic University of Leuven, Belgium.

Tutu, D. (1999), *No future without forgiveness*, London, Rider Books.

Umbreit, M. (1994), *Victim Meets Offender. The Impact of Restorative Justice and Mediation*, Monsey, Willow Tree Press.

Umbreit, M. Coates, R. B and Roberts, A. (1998), "Impact of victim-offender mediation in Canada, England and the United States". *The Crime Victims Report*, 20-92.

Umbreit, M. and Coates, R.B. (2001), "The Impact of Victim-Offender Mediation. Two Decades of Research", in Umbreit, M., *The Handbook of Victim-Offender Mediation. An Essential Guide to Practice and Research*, San Francisco, Jossey-Bass, 161-177.

Umbreit, M.S., Coates, R.B. and Vos, B. (2001), "Victim impact of meeting with young offenders: two decades of victim/offender mediation practice and research", in Morris, A. and Maxwell, G. (eds.), *Restorative justice for juveniles: conferencing, mediation and circles*, Oxford, Hart Publishing, 121-143.

Umbreit, M.S. and Roberts, A. (1994), *Mediation in Criminal Conflict in England: An Assessment of Services in Coventry and Leeds*, St. Paul, Minnesota, Center for Restorative Justice and Mediation.

United Nations (2002), *Basic principles on the use of restorative justice programmes in criminal matters*, UN Economic and Social Council.

Van Ness, D. (2003), "Proposed basic principles on the use of restorative justice: recognising the aims and limits of restorative justice", in von Hirsch, A., Roberts, J., Bottoms, A.E., Roach, K. and Schiff, M. (eds.), *Restorative justice and criminal justice: competing or reconcilable paradigms?*, Oxford, Hart Publishing, 157-176.

Weitekamp, E.G.M. (2001), "Mediation in Europe: paradoxes, problems and promises", in Morris, A. and Maxwell, G. (eds.), *Restorative justice for juveniles: conferencing, mediation and circles*, Oxford, Hart Publishing, 145-160.

Weitekamp, E.G.M. (2000), "Research on victim-offender mediation: findings and needs for the future", in European Forum for Victim-Offender Mediation and Restorative Justice (ed.), *Victim-offender mediation in Europe: making restorative justice work*, Leuven, Leuven University Press, 99-121.

Wright, M. (1996), *Justice for victims and offenders: a restorative response to crime,* Winchester, Watergate Press, 2nd edition.

Wright, M. (1989), "What the Public Wants", in Wright, M. and Galaway, B. (eds.), *Mediation and Criminal Justice. Victims, Offenders and Community*, London, SAGE Publications, 264-269.

Young, R. (2001), "Just cops doing 'shameful' business? Police-led restorative justice and the lessons of research", in Morris, A. and Maxwell, G. (eds.), *Restorative justice for juveniles: conferencing, mediation and circles*, Oxford, Hart Publishing, 195-226.

Zehr, H. (2002), *Little book of restorative justice*, Intercourse, PA, GoodBooks.

Zehr, H. (1995), *Changing lenses: a new focus for crime and justice*, Scottdale, PA, Herald Press, 2nd edition.

FURTHER READING

Bazemore, G. and Schiff, M. (eds.) (2001), *Restorative community justice. Repairing harm and transforming communities*, Cincinnatti, Anderson Publishing.

Bazemore, G. and Walgrave, L. (eds.) (1999), *Restorative Juvenile Justice: Repairing the Harm of Youth Crime*, Monsey, Criminal Justice Press.

Bieńkowska, E. (1999), *Poradnik mediatora: mediacja od A do Z, wzory pism, akty prawne*, Warszawa, Wydawnictwo Zrzeszenia Prawników Polskikh.

Cario, R. (ed.) (1997), *La médiation pénale. Entre répression et réparation*, Paris, L'Harmattan.

Chankova, D. (2002), *Mediatsiyata mezhdu zhertvata I izvershitelya na presteplenieto*, Sofia, Feneya (with English summary).

Crawford, A. and Newburn, T. (2003), *Youth offending and restorative justice. Implementing reform in youth justice*, Cullompton, Willan Publishing.

Czarnecka-Dzialuk, B. and Wójcik, D. (eds.) (1999), *Juvenile Offender-Victim mediation / Mediacja Nieletni przestepcy i ich ofiary*, Warsaw, Oficyna Naukowa (in English and Polish).

Czarnecka-Dzialuk, B. and Wójcik, D. (2001), *Mediacja w sprawach nieletnich w świetlee teorii i badań*, Warsaw, Typografika (with English summary).

Dignan, J. and Lowey, K. (2000), *Restorative justice. Options for Northern Ireland: A comparative review*, London, The Stationery Office Limited.

Dölling, D. u.a. (1998), *Täter-Opfer-Ausgleich in Deutschland. Bestandsaufnahme und Perspektiven*, Bonn, Forum Verlag Godesberg.

Faget, J. (1997), *La médiation. Essai de politique pénale*, Ramonville Saint-Agne, Erès.

Galaway, B. and Hudson, J. (eds.) (1996), *Restorative Justice: International Perspectives*, Monsey, Criminal Justice Press, 1996.

Graef, R. (2000), *Why restorative justice? Repairing the harm caused by crime*, London, Calouste Gulbenkian Foundation.

Hassemer, E., Marks, E. und Meyer, K. (eds.) (1997), *Zehn Jahre Täter-Opfer-Ausgleich und Konfliktschlichtung*, Bonn, Forum Verlag Godesberg.

Hudson, J., Morris, A., Maxwell, G. and Galaway, B. (eds.) (1996), *Family Group Conferences. Perspectives on Policy and Practice*, Monsey, Willow Tree Press.

Johnstone, G. (ed.) (2003), *A restorative justice reader. Texts, sources, context*, Cullompton, Willan Publishing.

Johnstone, G. (2002), *Restorative justice. Ideas, values, debates*, Cullompton, Willan Publishing.

Karnozova, L.M. (ed.), *Vosstanovitel'noe pravosudie dlya nesovershennoletnykh i sotsial'naya rabota: uchebnoe posobie*, Moscow, Tsentr "Sudebno-pravovaya Reforma" (with English summary).

Keeley, P. (2001), *Restorative justice. Challenges and Benefits For Irish Society*, Dublin, Victim/Offender Mediation Service.

Llewelynn, J.J. and Howse, R. (1998), *Restorative justice – A Conceptual Framework*, Ottawa, Law Commission of Canada.

Liebmann, M. (2000), *Mediation in context*, London, Jessica Kingsley Publishers.

McLaughlin, E., Fergusson, R., Hughes, G. and Westmarland, L. (eds.) (2003), *Restorative justice. Critical issues*, London, Sage Publications and Open University.

Mediation UK (1994), *Victim/offender mediation: guidelines for starting a service*, Bristol, Mediation UK.

Messmer, H. and Otto, H.-U. (eds.) (1992), *Restorative justice on trial. Pitfalls and potentials of victim-offender mediation – International research perspectives*, Dordrecht, Kluwer Academic Publishers.

Miers, D. (2001), *An International Review of Restorative Justice*, Crime Reduction Research Series Paper 10, London, Home Office.

O'Dwyer, K. (2001), *Restorative Justice Initiatives in the Garda Síochána. Evaluation of the Pilot Programme*, Templemore, Garda Research Unit.

Public Center for Legal and Judicial Reform (2001), *Restorative justice: the old civilization in the new Russia*, Moscow, Public Center for Legal and Judicial Reform.

Quill, D. and Wynne, J. (eds.) (1993), *Victim & Offender Mediation Handbook*, Bristol, Mediation UK.

Sharpe, S. (1998), *Restorative Justice: A Vision for Healing and Change*, Edmonton, Alberta, Edmonton Victim Offender Mediation Society.

Strang, H. and Braithwaite, J. (eds.) (2002), *Restorative justice and family violence*, Cambridge, Cambridge University Press.

Strang, H. and Braithwaite, J. (eds.) (2000), *Restorative justice. Philosophy to practice*, Aldershot, Ashgate.

Tsentr "Sudebno-pravovaya Reforma" (2001), *Vosstanovitel'noe pravosudie v Rossii: tekhnologiya vzaimodeistviya obshchestva i gosudarstva*, Moscow, Tsentr "Sudebno-pravovaya Reforma".

Umbreit, M. (2001), *The handbook of victim/offender mediation: an essential guide to practice and research*, San Fransisco, Jossey-Bass.

Van Ness, D. (1999), "Legal Issues of Restorative Justice", in Bazemore, G. and Walgrave, L. (eds.), *Restorative Juvenile Justice: Repairing the Harm of Youth Crime*, Monsey, Criminal Justice Press, 263-284.

Van Ness, D. and Strong, K.H. (1997), *Restoring Justice*, Cincinnati, Anderson Publishing Co., 1997.

Vanspauwen, K., Robert, L., Aertsen, I. and Parmentier, S. (2003), *Restorative justice and restorative detention. A selected and annotated bibliography*, Leuven, K. U. Leuven, Research Group Penology and Victimology.

von Hirsch, A., Roberts, J., Bottoms, A.E., Roach, K. and Schiff, M. (eds.) (2003), *Restorative justice and criminal justice: competing or reconcilable paradigms*, Oxford, Hart Publishing.

Walgrave, L. (ed.) (2003), *Repositioning restorative justice*, Cullompton, Willan Publishing.

Walgrave, L. (ed.) (2002), *Restorative justice and the law*, Cullompton, Willan Publishing.

Weitekamp, E.G.M. and Kerner, H.-J. (eds.) (2002), *Restorative justice. Theoretical foundations*, Cullompton, Willan Publishing.

Weitekamp, E.G.M. and Kerner, H.-J. (eds.) (2003), *Restorative justice in context. International practice and directions*, Cullompton, Willan Publishing.

Wemmers, J.-A. and Canuto, M. (2002), *Victims' Experiences with, Expectations and Perceptions of Restorative Justice: A Critical Review of the Literature – draft*, Ottawa, Department of Justice Canada.

Wright, M. (1999), *Restoring respect for justice: a symposium*, Winchester, Waterside Press.

PUBLICATIONS BY THE INTEGRATED PROJECT "RESPONSES TO VIOLENCE IN EVERYDAY LIFE IN A DEMOCRATIC SOCIETY"

Urban crime prevention – a guide for local authorities (2002)
ISBN 92-871-4943-7

The prevention of violence in sport (2002)
ISBN 92-871-5038-9

Facets of interculturality in education (2003)
ISBN 92-871-5088-5

Towards a migration management strategy (2003)

Security and democracy under pressure of violence (2003)
ISBN 92-871-5201-2

Violence, conflict and intercultural dialogue (2003)
ISBN 92-871-5251-9

Violence in schools – a challenge for the local community (2003)
ISBN 92-871-5326-4

New patterns of irregular migration (2003)
ISBN 92-871-5626-4

Prevention of violence against women (2003)
ISBN 92-871-5291-8

For more information:

"Responses to violence in everyday life in a democratic society"
Website: http://www.coe.int/violence

European Forum for Victim-Offender Mediation and Restorative Justice
Hooverplein 10
3000 Leuven
Belgium
Tel.: +32 16 32 54 29
Fax: +32 16 32 54 74
E-mail: info@euforumrj.org
http://www.euforumrj.org

Sales agents for publications of the Council of Europe
Agents de vente des publications du Conseil de l'Europe

AUSTRALIA/AUSTRALIE
Hunter Publications, 58A, Gipps Street
AUS-3066 COLLINGWOOD, Victoria
Tel.: (61) 3 9417 5361
Fax: (61) 3 9419 7154
E-mail: Sales@hunter-pubs.com.au
http://www.hunter-pubs.com.au

BELGIUM/BELGIQUE
La Librairie européenne SA
50, avenue A. Jonnart
B-1200 BRUXELLES 20
Tel.: (32) 2 734 0281
Fax: (32) 2 735 0860
E-mail: info@libeurop.be
http://www.libeurop.be

Jean de Lannoy
202, avenue du Roi
B-1190 BRUXELLES
Tel.: (32) 2 538 4308
Fax: (32) 2 538 0841
E-mail: jean.de.lannoy@euronet.be
http://www.jean-de-lannoy.be

CANADA
Renouf Publishing Company Limited
5369 Chemin Canotek Road
CDN-OTTAWA, Ontario, K1J 9J3
Tel.: (1) 613 745 2665
Fax: (1) 613 745 7660
E-mail: order.dept@renoufbooks.com
http://www.renoufbooks.com

**CZECH REPUBLIC/
RÉPUBLIQUE TCHÈQUE**
Suweco Cz Dovoz Tisku Praha
Ceskomoravska 21
CZ-18021 PRAHA 9
Tel.: (420) 2 660 35 364
Fax: (420) 2 683 30 42
E-mail: import@suweco.cz

DENMARK/DANEMARK
GAD Direct
Fiolstaede 31-33
DK-1171 COPENHAGEN K
Tel.: (45) 33 13 72 33
Fax: (45) 33 12 54 94
E-mail: info@gaddirect.dk

FINLAND/FINLANDE
Akateeminen Kirjakauppa
Keskuskatu 1, PO Box 218
FIN-00381 HELSINKI
Tel.: (358) 9 121 41
Fax: (358) 9 121 4450
E-mail: akatilaus@stockmann.fi
http://www.akatilaus.akateeminen.com

FRANCE
La Documentation française
(Diffusion/Vente France entière)
124, rue H. Barbusse
F-93308 AUBERVILLIERS Cedex
Tel.: (33) 01 40 15 70 00
Fax: (33) 01 40 15 68 00
E-mail: commandes.vel@ladocfrancaise.gouv.fr
http://www.ladocfrancaise.gouv.fr

Librairie Kléber (Vente Strasbourg)
Palais de l'Europe
F-67075 STRASBOURG Cedex
Fax: (33) 03 88 52 91 21
E-mail: librairie.kleber@coe.int

**GERMANY/ALLEMAGNE
AUSTRIA/AUTRICHE**
UNO Verlag
Am Hofgarten 10
D-53113 BONN
Tel.: (49) 2 28 94 90 20
Fax: (49) 2 28 94 90 222
E-mail: bestellung@uno-verlag.de
http://www.uno-verlag.de

GREECE/GRÈCE
Librairie Kauffmann
28, rue Stadiou
GR-ATHINAI 10564
Tel.: (30) 1 32 22 160
Fax: (30) 1 32 30 320
E-mail: ord@otenet.gr

HUNGARY/HONGRIE
Euro Info Service
Hungexpo Europa Kozpont ter 1
H-1101 BUDAPEST
Tel.: (361) 264 8270
Fax: (361) 264 8271
E-mail: euroinfo@euroinfo.hu
http://www.euroinfo.hu

ITALY/ITALIE
Libreria Commissionaria Sansoni
Via Duca di Calabria 1/1, CP 552
I-50125 FIRENZE
Tel.: (39) 556 4831
Fax: (39) 556 41257
E-mail: licosa@licosa.com
http://www.licosa.com

NETHERLANDS/PAYS-BAS
De Lindeboom Internationale Publikaties
PO Box 202, MA de Ruyterstraat 20 A
NL-7480 AE HAAKSBERGEN
Tel.: (31) 53 574 0004
Fax: (31) 53 572 9296
E-mail: books@delindeboom.com
http://home-1-worldonline.nl/~lindeboo/

NORWAY/NORVÈGE
Akademika, A/S Universitetsbokhandel
PO Box 84, Blindern
N-0314 OSLO
Tel.: (47) 22 85 30 30
Fax: (47) 23 12 24 20

POLAND/POLOGNE
Głowna Księgarnia Naukowa
im. B. Prusa
Krakowskie Przedmiescie 7
PL-00-068 WARSZAWA
Tel.: (48) 29 22 66
Fax: (48) 22 26 64 49
E-mail: inter@internews.com.pl
http://www.internews.com.pl

PORTUGAL
Livraria Portugal
Rua do Carmo, 70
P-1200 LISBOA
Tel.: (351) 13 47 49 82
Fax: (351) 13 47 02 64
E-mail: liv.portugal@mail.telepac.pt

SPAIN/ESPAGNE
Mundi-Prensa Libros SA
Castelló 37
E-28001 MADRID
Tel.: (34) 914 36 37 00
Fax: (34) 915 75 39 98
E-mail: libreria@mundiprensa.es
http://www.mundiprensa.com

SWITZERLAND/SUISSE
Adeco – Van Diermen
Chemin du Lacuez 41
CH-1807 BLONAY
Tel.: (41) 21 943 26 73
Fax: (41) 21 943 36 05
E-mail: info@adeco.org

UNITED KINGDOM/ROYAUME-UNI
TSO (formerly HMSO)
51 Nine Elms Lane
GB-LONDON SW8 5DR
Tel.: (44) 207 873 8372
Fax: (44) 207 873 8200
E-mail: customer.services@theso.co.uk
http://www.the-stationery-office.co.uk
http://www.itsofficial.net

**UNITED STATES and CANADA/
ÉTATS-UNIS et CANADA**
Manhattan Publishing Company
2036 Albany Post Road
CROTON-ON-HUDSON,
NY 10520, USA
Tel.: (1) 914 271 5194
Fax: (1) 914 271 5856
E-mail: Info@manhattanpublishing.com
http://www.manhattanpublishing.com

Council of Europe Publishing/Editions du Conseil de l'Europe
F-67075 Strasbourg Cedex
Tel.: (33) 03 88 41 25 81 – Fax: (33) 03 88 41 39 10 – E-mail: publishing@coe.int – Website: http://book.coe.int